Sensory and Motor Strategies
3rd Edition

SENSORY AND MOTOR STRATEGIES
3rd Edition

Practical Ways to Help Autistic Children
and Young People Learn and Achieve

CORINNA LAURIE
Illustrated by Kirsteen Wright

Jessica Kingsley Publishers
London and Philadelphia

First edition published in 2013 by The National Autistic Society

This edition published in Great Britain in 2022 by Jessica Kingsley Publishers
An imprint of Hodder & Stoughton Ltd
An Hachette Company

4

Front cover images source: Kirsteen Wright.

A CIP catalogue record for this title is available from the British Library and the Library of Congress

ISBN 978 1 83997 272 0
eISBN 978 1 83997 271 3

Printed and bound by CPI Group (UK) Ltd, Croydon, CR0 4YY

Jessica Kingsley Publishers' policy is to use papers that are natural, renewable and recyclable products and made from wood grown in sustainable forests. The logging and manufacturing processes are expected to conform to the environmental regulations of the country of origin.

Jessica Kingsley Publishers
Carmelite House
50 Victoria Embankment
London EC4Y 0DZ

www.jkp.com

Contents

• • • • • • • • • • • • •

Introduction 7

SENSORY STRATEGIES

Arousal states 13
The under-aroused student 13
'Shut down' students 14
The sensory-seeking student 14
The over-aroused student 14
In summary 15

Self-regulation 16
Zones of Regulation 17
Energy accounting 19
Regulation/Emotion scales 19

Easy environmental modifications . . . 21
Lighting and vision 21
Noise 21
Smell 22

Calming strategies 23

The touch system 25
Touch (tactile) hypersensitivity and hyposensitivity 26
Behaviour you may notice 26
Strategies for students who are sensitive to touch 27

The gustatory system 31
Gustatory (oral) hypersensitivity 32
Gustatory (oral) hyposensitivity 32
Strategies for 'picky' eaters with gustatory hypersensitivity 33
Strategies for gustatory hyposensitivity 34

The auditory system 35
Hypersensitivity to sound (auditory defensiveness) 36

Hyposensitivity to sound 36
Strategies for students who are sensitive to sound 37
Strategies for students who are under-responsive to sound 38
Strategies for students with auditory processing differences 38

The olfactory system 39
Hypersensitivity to smell 39
Hyposensitivity to smell 40
Strategies for hyper-/hypo-responsiveness 40
Aromatherapy in the classroom 41

The visual system 43
Behaviour you may notice 43
Strategies to help visually under-stimulated students 44
Strategies to help visually over-stimulated students 44

The vestibular system 46
Behaviour you may notice 47
Strategies for students who are hypersensitive to movement 47
Strategies for students who seek increased vestibular input 48

The proprioceptive system 49
Behaviour you may notice 50
Strategies for students with poor proprioception 50

The interoceptive system 53
Over-responsive 54
Under-responsive 54
Strategies 54

MOTOR SKILLS STRATEGIES

Motor skills overview. 59
   Gross motor skills 59
   Core/postural stability 60
   Balance 62
   Body awareness/spatial awareness 62

Objectives of yoga sessions 64

Core stability. 66

Fine motor skills. 68

Visual motor integration. 70
   Compensatory strategies 70
   Activities to improve visual motor
   integration 71

Visual perception 73
   Strategies 74
   Activities to help improve visual
   perception 75

Handwriting. 77
   Prerequisite skills required for
   handwriting 77
   Sequence of handwriting development 78
   Pencil grip development 78
   Pre-writing shapes 78
   General tips for success 79

Scissor skills 80
   Prerequisites for skilled scissor use 80
   What scissors to use? 80
   Activity ideas to improve cutting skills 81

Cutlery skills 83

Dressing milestones. 84
   Activities/strategies to support
   dressing skills 85

Simple strategies for secondary school
students. 87

PHOTOCOPIABLE RESOURCES

Sensory treasure chest 91
Sensory sensitivity checklist 92
Messy play 94
Food play activities 96
Movement break ideas 98
Scooter board activities 100
Daily sensory sessions 101
Proprioception – younger students 104
Proprioception – older students 106
Vestibular activities 108
Calming activities 110
Fidget toys 111
Core stability 112
Progressive muscle relaxation 115
Relaxation yoga 116
Self joint compressions 118
Infinity walk 119
Scooter board activities 120
Therapy gym ball activities 122
Fine motor skills activities 125
Bilateral coordination
(using two hands) 126
Multisensory approach to
handwriting 127
Handwriting warm-up 129
Putty ideas for hand strengthening 131
Buttons made easy 132
Zip practice 133
Shoelace tying 134

References and further reading 137

About the author 139

INTRODUCTION

M ost of us unconsciously learn to combine our senses (sight, sound, smell, touch, taste, balance and the sense of our body in space) in order to make sense of our environment. However, this is often not the case for autistic children and young people who may have difficulty filtering information to prevent it from becoming overwhelming, uncomfortable and/or painful. On the flip side, some autistic people actively seek sensory sensations to relieve anxiety, to calm and often just for pleasure and relaxation. Sensory processing differences can be described as experiencing particular sensory stimuli differently from the neurotypical population.

Differences in sensory responses were included in the 2013 update of the *Diagnostic and Statistical Manual of Mental Disorders (DSM-5)* (American Psychiatric Association 2013), a manual used by clinicians to make an autism diagnosis.

Research and my clinical observations over the years have highlighted that many autistic children or those with sensory processing differences often have concurrent difficulties with posture, coordination and motor planning. This book contains sections to identify and help reduce the impact of these difficulties to improve functional abilities and remove barriers for children and young people to achieve their aspirations.

Jean Ayres, an occupational therapist and founder of Sensory Integration Therapy, said:

> The brain locates, sorts and orders sensations, somewhat like the way a traffic light directs moving cars. When sensations flow in a well-organized or integrated manner, the brain uses those sensations to form perceptions, behaviours and learning. When the flow of sensations is disorganized, life can be like a rush-hour traffic jam. (Ayres 1979, p.5)

Parents, teachers and support workers everywhere will be very aware of children and young people who experience difficulties regulating and modulating certain sensory sensations. It can affect their emotional state and their ability to access both the curriculum and daily life. If reasonable adjustments are not made for these students, it can negatively affect their wellbeing. It is my opinion that reasonable adjustments to take positive steps to ensure that all students can fully participate in education and life choices are an essential part of our role as professionals, care-givers and educators.

Making sure a student with sensory processing differences has the right sensory opportunities – often referred to as a 'sensory diet' – infused throughout their day will remove barriers to learning and go some way to improve their wellbeing. A sensory diet provides scheduled activities and sensory input for the body and neurological system. Just as our bodies need food evenly spaced throughout the day, so they need activities to keep their arousal levels optimal and modulated. When this happens, students are in a better position to be successful learners and happy individuals.

> Roughly 40% of autistic people have symptoms of at least one anxiety disorder at any time, compared with up to 15% in the general population. (National Autistic Society 2020a)

As an occupational therapist with a particular interest (actually, it's a passion!) in sensory processing and motor differences, I hope this book will allow you to identify possible challenges, recognise signs of overload and work in a co-productive way with your student to develop sensory regulation strategies, improve motor skills and well-being, and provide you with a variety of practical strategies to help regulate children and young people's sensory processing and allow them to function at their optimal arousal level. It should help reduce anxiety and have a positive impact on that student's life as a whole.

> And most importantly: Do not judge or question an autistic person's sensory experience or need for sensory tools. (Jamie Knight (n.d.))

The great thing about accommodating a student with sensory processing differences in the classroom is that all students can benefit from sensory strategies, techniques and activities. They increase focus and attention, and allow students to be ready to learn and to achieve. Simple environmental adaptations, including how we present ourselves around our students, will ultimately improve the outcome for all.

In the words of Jolene Stockman (2019), 'It's not "autism-friendly" to make our lives more peaceful, it's human-friendly.'

SENSORY PROCESSING DIFFERENCES AND AUTISM

Autism is a lifelong developmental disability that affects how people perceive the world and interact with others. It is a spectrum condition and is sometimes referred to as an autism spectrum disorder, or an ASD.

Autistic people may share difficulties, but being autistic will affect them in different ways. Some autistic people also have additional learning disabilities, mental health issues or other conditions (like anyone), meaning people need different levels of support for their neurodiversity.

All those with neurodiversity deserve the support and adaptions required to positively impact their lives and ensure acceptance becomes the norm.

It is thought that about two-thirds of autistic people have sensory processing differences. People on the autism spectrum can be hypersensitive or hyposensitive to one or more of the seven senses: sound, vision, touch, taste, smell, the vestibular system and the proprioceptive system. Some may move between hyper- and hyposensitivity.

If a person is hypersensitive, they might, for example, see lights a lot brighter or hear sounds a lot louder than others. If a person is hyposensitive, they may have difficulty processing certain stimuli and so seek them out. For example, a person who is hyposensitive to sound may make loud noises as a way of stimulating their underactive sense.

SENSORY STRATEGIES

AROUSAL STATES

If you and your colleagues work with students with a sensory processing difference, it is important to make sure that you have a good understanding of different 'arousal states', their presentation and ways in which these states can be modulated so that students can focus, learn and achieve.

All students present differently, and some students' arousal levels and modulation rates change regularly throughout the day depending on their mood, the environment, hunger levels and so on.

There are several factors that will/can affect our arousal levels such as:

- environmental considerations
- sensory differences
- communication differences and challenges
- wellbeing.

If these critical factors are not considered, then the 'CAFÉ effect' could occur – a term coined by Joanne Neill Smith, Clinical Lead Speech and Language Therapist at the National Autistic Society (NAS).

- **C**onfusion
- **A**nxiety
- **F**ear
- **E**xhaustion

● THE UNDER-AROUSED STUDENT

Students with low arousal levels can demonstrate a wide range of behaviour. They may become fatigued during what they perceive to be mundane activities, such as listening to a teacher, watching a screen or completing lengthy worksheets.

They may yawn excessively, have a glazed look in their eyes, appear to lack motivation or actually fall asleep at their desk. They are often observed to be slumped in their chair staring into space.

Under-aroused students may also use fidgety or sensory-seeking behaviour in an attempt to stay alert and organised. These students need alerting and vestibular activities to 'wake up' the brain stem. This will help an individual student to achieve an optimal zone for interacting with their world for up to two hours. (See **'Movement break ideas'** and **'Vestibular activities'** in the **Photocopiable resources** section.)

● 'SHUT DOWN' STUDENTS

A student may present as under-aroused outwardly but is in fact what we term as 'shut down'.

This often happens with students who have sensory differences in one or more sensory systems – that is, they are overly sensitive to something like touch, light or sound.

Shutdown is the brain's way of protecting itself against becoming completely overwhelmed. If a student is shut down, they may appear to be under-aroused. However, if you present alerting activities to an under-aroused student, the response would be an increase in their state of alertness. In an individual who is in 'shutdown', this will not happen; in fact, they are so over-aroused that their brain has stopped registering sensory information. They will continue to appear under-aroused.

If you have tried alerting or vestibular activities and they have not helped, it is vital to carry out activities that are related to calming and proprioception (see **'Calming activities'**, **'Proprioception – younger students'** and **'Proprioception – older students'** in the **Photocopiable resources** section) to reduce anxiety and overload. These activities will help to inhibit the brain's firing of neurons, which will be overwhelming the student. They will, therefore, have the chance to become calm and regain their optimal state of arousal.

● THE SENSORY-SEEKING STUDENT

Students who are sensory seekers need to be stimulated by things in their environment in order to regulate themselves. They have decreased natural sensitivity to sensory input and therefore must seek increased sensations in order to 'feel' or gain feedback. These are the students who constantly fidget, run off, seek out messy activities and appear to crash around the classroom.

It is a good idea to offer substitutes to sensory-seeking students so that they receive sensory input in a more appropriate manner. Timetabled movement breaks may reduce instances of fidgeting and running off. Alternative dynamic seating such as ball chairs, wobble stools and wobble cushions will provide acceptable fidgety movement, and fidget toys will also help to answer this need. In addition, it is often helpful to engage sensory-seeking students in as much physical play as possible!

● THE OVER-AROUSED STUDENT

Students who are over-aroused are often sensory-sensitive and quickly overwhelmed. They will have great difficulty screening out environmental distractions and can therefore find it extremely hard to concentrate. These students often appear to be explosive and controlling. They have difficulty working in a group, can be disruptive and find transition and any change of routine challenging. These students need a calming and low-arousal classroom environment so that they can concentrate on learning. 'Transitions of any type can be difficult for many autistic people. These can seem very minor changes to us but the impact on autistic people can be substantial' (Beadle-Brown and Mills 2018, p.20).

● IN SUMMARY

When working with students with sensory processing differences, our main aim is for our students to feel 'just right'. They will then be able to focus on the task at hand rather than being distracted or made anxious by environmental stimuli.

This book contains a number of strategies and recommendations that are general in nature. It is strongly recommended that you work with an occupational therapist who specialises in treating individuals with sensory processing differences for individualised intervention programmes.

Students with sensory processing differences run on very high levels of anxiety and their behaviour may appear to reflect this. It is crucial to gain an insight into the child or young person's world and work together with them to find helpful strategies. We should never judge the 'behaviour' but instead try to understand, empathise and work together to make adjustments to assist regulation. Some students need to use sensory stimulation to regulate and calm themselves. Instead of avoiding this, you should ensure there are opportunities, environmental spaces and a shared understanding of the importance and benefit to the child or young person. Some autistic children and adults use 'stimming' (repetitive movements such as hand flapping, rocking or finger flicking) to calm, re-regulate and for enjoyment, and this should be accepted not challenged. In the words of Agony Autie (2018):

> Stimming is a great way to combat sensory inputs because the stim helps to 'block the inputs'. So, it helps with regulation.

It may be necessary to timetable certain activities if a student needs to use these activities to calm. Attempting to remove the activity completely may simply exacerbate anxiety and lead to meltdown. To give an example: many of us will know from experience that being on a strict diet means that all you can think about is food!

It should be remembered: 'A meltdown is not the same as a tantrum. It is when a person becomes completely overwhelmed and is unable to function in an environment' (Steward 2020).

> Like canaries in a coal mine, the sensory defensive should stand as a warning that sensory overload is dangerous for everyone. It impairs concentration, increases irritability and vulnerability to illness, decreases quality of life and pushes everyone to levels of stress unknown before modern technology. (Heller 2003, p.10)

I hope that you find the strategies in this book simple and effective. They generally do not cost much. Have fun with them and remember that they will help students to maintain their optimum arousal state, promote confidence and improve self-esteem.

SELF-REGULATION

Self-regulation requires the ability to recognise behaviours and emotions and successfully adapt and use strategies to meet the demands of any situation, to prevent burnout/meltdown and to decrease stress, anxiety and fatigue.

Temple Grandin (2016) defines self-regulation as 'the skill of managing feelings so that they don't reach overwhelming levels and interfere with learning and development'.

The ultimate aim is to help the person reduce excess activation in the nervous system that would otherwise result in a fight-or-flight response, shutdown or increased anxiety.

Self-regulation generally falls into three categories, although these are often intertwined:

- sensory regulation
- emotional regulation
- cognitive regulation.

Poor self-regulation can cause extreme fatigue and exhaustion, which is often exacerbated for our autistic students by:

- sensory overload
- dealing with social situations
- masking or camouflaging their autistic traits
- suppressing stimming
- a sense of not meeting other people's/society's expectations of them.

Changes in routines or day-to-day life, such as a change of school or job, can increase anxiety and can be additional causes for autistic fatigue and burnout (NAS 2021).

Given the complexities surrounding self-regulation, it is key to utilise a transdisciplinary approach (this means everyone who is actively involved in supporting the child) with the child at the centre to identify and address the underlying 'stressors' for optimal outcomes.

It is important for us to work with children and young people to:

- increase understanding of emotional literacy (it isn't possible to use self-regulation techniques without an ability to recognise and understand emotions)

- increase self-awareness and recognise the signs in their own bodies when sensory or emotional overload begins
- identify their specific triggers (sensory, emotional and cognitive)
- communicate their feelings effectively
- select effective coping strategies.

There are many differing methods to support self-regulation, and it is important to work in collaboration with the child or young person to establish a method that works for them. Three commonly used tools are the Zones of Regulation, energy accounting and regulation/emotion scales.

Whatever strategy/tool is felt to be useful, it is vital that the child or young person is offered time off and time to rest and recuperate.

Time off from work or school and other high-stress activities is key to managing stress levels. Ensuring time for activities/interests that re-energise and promote relaxation is key. (NAS 2020a)

So often autistic people feel the need to hide or mask their autistic traits in public, and this can be exhausting. It is therefore important to factor times into your child's/student's day for things like stimming/repetitive behaviours and taking part in activities that are important to them. This will reduce the build-up of stress and anxiety that may lead to fatigue and meltdown when at home in their 'safe space'.

● ZONES OF REGULATION

The Zones of Regulation curriculum was developed by Leah Kuypers, an occupational therapist from the United States. Leah developed the curriculum to target the underlying causes of dysregulation rather than negatively focusing on the outward 'behaviour'. To implement this curriculum, it is important to seek training and purchase the required resources.

The Zones of Regulation framework is based on the premise that self-regulation requires the integration of many neurologically based skills. These include sensory processing and modulation, emotional regulation, executive functioning, language processing, pragmatic language, perspective taking, social cognition and central coherence.

The techniques and Zones focus on self-control, building emotional resiliency, self-management, impulse control and sensory regulation.

There are four Zones included in the Zones of Regulation, and each Zone has its own colour. Each of the Zones is based on a set of feelings/emotions/energy levels. Within these Zones, the child or young person should be supported to select tools from their individualised 'toolkit/toolbox' to aid regulation.

- The **Red Zone** describes extremely heightened states of alertness and intense emotions, including anger, rage, intense sadness and feeling out of control. These are the emotions associated with a fight-or-flight response.

- The **Yellow Zone** describes elevated emotions and heightened emotional states. These emotions can be negative or positive, including anxiety, stress, nervousness, excitement and restlessness.
- In the **Green Zone**, a person feels calm and alert. Common emotional states include happiness, contentment, calmness, readiness to learn and readiness to communicate.
- The **Blue Zone** describes low states of alertness. Typical emotions experienced in this state include sadness, boredom, feeling unwell and exhaustion. A person may feel tired or depressed while in this Zone or be in shutdown.

How does it work?

I strongly recommend completing training with Leah (training schedule available at Zonesofregulation.com) to fully understand how to implement the Zones of Regulation curriculum.

Students need first to be able to identify and label internal states and emotions in themselves and be able to communicate this to others. This will enable them to identify the Zone they are in and subsequently strategies/tools to assist self-regulation and move between the Zones.

The aim is for our children and young people to be able to take control of this for themselves, aiding their functional independence and occupational performance (OT jargon alert!).

In practice, I have found it beneficial to target Zones to motivating and clearly recognisable/tangible subjects. Examples of these are easily found using search engines and include characters from the Disney/Pixar film *Inside Out*, modes of transport (from bicycle to Ferrari) and Mr. Men and Little Miss characters for each Zone.

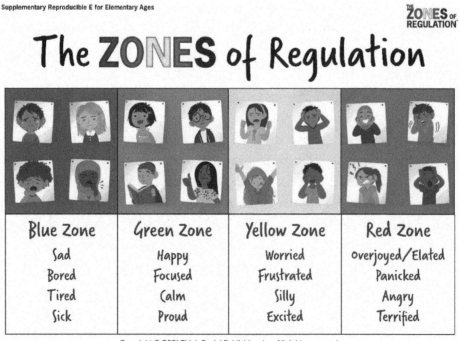

Supplementary Reproducible E for Elementary Ages

The ZONES of Regulation

Blue Zone	Green Zone	Yellow Zone	Red Zone
Sad	Happy	Worried	Overjoyed/Elated
Bored	Focused	Frustrated	Panicked
Tired	Calm	Silly	Angry
Sick	Proud	Excited	Terrified

Source: Kuypers 2011. (See https://library.jkp.com/ redeem for a full-colour version of this image.)

● ENERGY ACCOUNTING

If the child or young person you care for is experiencing fatigue or burnout, helping them to manage their energy levels is essential, and energy accounting is a great way to do this.

Energy accounting is a simple method that works by sitting down with the child or young person and creating a long list of things that drain energy from them (withdrawals) and replenish energy in them (deposits) to prevent burnout.

The idea is that when a withdrawal is made, or numerous withdrawals are made, deposits also have to be made in order to prevent the account running into debt, which can trigger a meltdown, increase anxiety and damage wellbeing.

Withdrawals	Deposits
Putting on school uniform (50)	iPad time (60)
Noisy taxi ride (60)	Time with school dog (50)
Lasagne for lunch (20)	Time in school 'calm room' (40)
After-school club (50)	Alone time in bedroom (50)
180	200

Some people prefer to use a pictorial image such as depleting battery life or gaming lives. Again, this needs to be personalised and carried out regularly to be effective.

There are now apps readily available to support energy accounting which have been created by autistic young people and adults.

● REGULATION/EMOTION SCALES

The 5-point scale originally developed by Kari Dunn Buron is a self-management tool. Similar to other self-management strategies, it is a visual system that can help to organise a person's thinking when working through challenging situations, particularly those that require social understanding.

Social anxiety, catastrophising and differences in social understanding can make it difficult for a person to work through emotions.

Creating a predictable and structured visual system for working through challenging situations can be beneficial to work through solutions.

A scale can be created using colours, pictures or a rating system of 1 to 5, with 1 being something that is not a concern and 5 being something that causes stress, upset and possibly meltdown. Used in conjunction with an anxiety curve (Buron and Curtis 2012), this can track triggers for a variety of situations and visually illustrate the power of anxiety and its influence on behaviour.

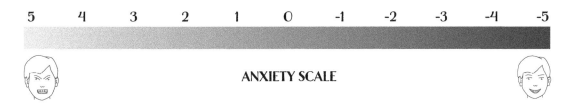

ANXIETY SCALE

A regulation/emotion scale, once learned, gives students a supported voice to talk about feelings – for example, 'I'm feeling like a 3; I better take a break.' The scale gives the opportunities throughout the day to frame conversations around feelings in a structured and visual manner.

The scale can also be used to help children and young people to link how they feel with strategies to try to reduce their level of stress, voice volume, anxiety, etc. Simply use one of the columns to write/draw actions in. It is again super important that this is a collaborative process, with the child or young person's voice at the centre of the approach.

For all of these self-regulation tools and techniques, it is crucial to remember that these need to be introduced at a time of calm and when the child feels ready and supported.

EASY ENVIRONMENTAL MODIFICATIONS

Symptoms of sensory processing differences are often exacerbated by the physical environment at school, in the classroom and at home. Many environmental factors cannot be controlled, but here are a few quick ideas for making an environment less stressful.

LIGHTING AND VISION

- Take regular breaks in which you ask all students to close their eyes for 60 seconds.
- Turn off lights when not needed. Avoid fluorescent lights where possible. Instead, open curtains and blinds to make use of natural light. Adjustable blinds are also a good idea.
- Consider using tinted window film.
- Use buff-coloured paper and a background when using a whiteboard.
- Change the background colour on the whiteboard/computer to reduce visual stress.
- Reduce the amount of artwork or other items on the walls.
- Provide a privacy screen so that students can have their own area.
- Provide clear pencil cases to aid organisation and reduce panicky rooting around for pens and pencils.

NOISE

- Control noise by keeping doors and windows closed when necessary.
- Carpeting, curtains and blinds can help to absorb noise.
- Some students could wear ear defenders/ear buds, or you could use background music to muffle external sounds.
- Place felt pads under furniture legs to reduce dragging sounds.
- Think about using tables with chairs attached to reduce the scraping in and out sound.

● SMELL

- Reduce the amount of perfume, body lotions and other scented cosmetics that staff may use.
- Consider what outside smells might be present and adjust the environment accordingly. For example, if the grass has recently been mown, keep the windows closed.
- Allow students to use alternative toilet facilities if they perceive the nearest one to be too smelly.
- Suggest students wear a towelling wrist band and or carry a handkerchief with a preferred smell on (e.g. Mum's perfume). This can be used to aid calm and block out other smells.
- Consider using an aromatherapy burner to mask smells. See the section **'Aromatherapy in the classroom'**.

CALMING STRATEGIES

In this chapter we'll look at some simple ways to help students to stay calm.

The things that you can do yourself include keeping your voice calm and rhythmic, and providing students with easier means of communicating with you. Students who are in overload may not be able to articulate their frustration, so give them ways in which they can tell you they're feeling stressed and need time out. Examples include an emotion thermometer, 5-point scale, Zones of Regulation, Amazing Awareness Bands (see **www.amazingawarenessbands.co.uk**) and packs of coloured cards in which a particular colour indicates that a student needs a break.

Here are some other ideas for calming strategies.

- Use natural lighting whenever possible and try to avoid fluorescent lights. Avoid seating visually sensitive students next to windows or in sun traps.
- Allow the use of stress balls or fidget toys while students are listening or doing work while seated. Blu Tack and fidget cubes work well for older children.
- Set achievable targets so that students don't feel rushed.
- Allow frequent changes of position and scheduled movement breaks (see '**Movement break ideas**' in the **Photocopiable resources** section). These should happen at least once every hour for primary school students.
- Clearly denote the passage of time. Use timers, sand timers and iPad apps to show time and therefore a clear ending to an activity.
- Provide 'heavy work' activities (see '**Proprioception – younger students**' and '**Proprioception – older students**' in the **Photocopiable resources** section).
- Allow students to wear headphones or ear defenders if they are bothered or distracted by background noise. If students are listening to music, give them choice over what they listen to; different people may find different music relaxing. Music with a steady rhythm will improve focus and attention.
- Use visual supports such as timetables, emotion thermometers and 'now and next' cards to prepare students and provide structure. These can help students to feel less anxious as they know what will be happening next.
- Provide a 'sanctuary' area where over-stimulated students can go to escape. This could be a pop-up tent or simply a blanket over a table. Put a large beanbag inside and some sensory toys. Rocking chairs also work well for some students.
- Encourage students to keep a sports water bottle with them. Sucking is calming and helps focus.

- Allow students to chew gum or chewy sweets during times of prolonged concentration, as these can also help to maintain focus.
- Minimise visual distractions such as posters and signs in the classroom. Consider using one colour as a border on all posters for consistency.
- Allow dynamic seating, such as ball chairs, rocking stools and wobble cushions. These will allow students to fidget and help to maintain concentration.
- When seated on the floor, define boundaries/personal space by getting students to sit in a hoop, on a section of carpet tiles or on a small rug.
- Consider the use of weighted equipment such as lap pads, weighted waistcoats and shoulder wraps. Weighted garments provide deep pressure which calms the nervous system.
- Define students' desk boundaries by providing a privacy screen or taping defined space on desk.
- Use clear pencil cases to aid organisation.
- Provide post-it notes to doodle on or jot down things to remember. This reduces anxiety.

THE TOUCH SYSTEM

Our sense of touch allows us to feel the world around us and plays a vital role in everything we do, whether at school, at home or during leisure and playtime. The tactile system is designed to alert us to threats, to give our body boundaries and, when combined with the proprioceptive sense (see **'The proprioceptive system'** below), to give us body image and self-awareness.

Our tactile system is located in the nerves supplying our skin. These nerves send information to the brain.

Unlike other senses such as vision or hearing, our sense of touch is not limited to certain parts of the body but exists all over – including in our mouths. This makes it one of the most difficult systems to target in students with sensory sensitivity.

Our sense of touch is varied and subtle; through our skin, we can sense the general temperature, whether a particular object is hot or cold, and if the weather is windy or calm. Through our hands, we can touch another person, pick up and explore an object, and understand how much force it can withstand. Our sense of touch allows us to be gentle when picking up an egg or firm when picking up a heavy book.

The tactile sense gives us information about our environment and the qualities of objects within it. It can tell us about the consistency or texture of something (whether it is hard, soft, sharp or dull) and about the temperature (if it is hot or cold), and it can tell us if something causes us to feel pain.

It also plays an important role in our basic survival by helping us to decide if we need to engage our protective systems, such as the 'fight or flight or freeze' response. For example, it is activated when a wasp or spider lands on our skin.

We all experience a degree of hypersensitivity (over-sensitivity) to touch when we are unwell. For instance, our skin can feel sore when we have flu.

Some students who have sensory processing differences feel this all the time, especially with light touch, which can feel painful and genuinely uncomfortable. Experiencing this response to everyday sensations and being in a constant state of high arousal with high levels of adrenaline in the body can cause fatigue, burnout and exhaustion.

These students will often describe their clothes as feeling like sandpaper. They will notice every lump, bump and crease in their clothing and often prefer to be naked as a result.

It is important to know that these students are not 'making a fuss' but are genuinely finding a sensation painful.

We are assaulted with sensory stimuli from all directions and find it difficult to filter out information we don't need... The filters in our brains are filled with holes which let in far too much information. (Beale-Ellis 2017, p.23)

The noise feels like someone has a knife and has sliced off the top of my head, exposing my brain, which feels like a balloon, ready to burst. (Limpsfield Grange School and Martin 2015, p.43)

Temple Grandin also recounted her sensitivity to touch:

I ached to be loved-hugged [but] even being touched by the teacher made me flinch and draw back. Wanting but withdrawing. My brain-damaged nervous system imprisoned me. It was as if a sliding glass door separated me from the world of love and human understanding. (Grandin 1986, p.32)

TOUCH (TACTILE) HYPERSENSITIVITY AND HYPOSENSITIVITY

A student who is **hypersensitive** to touch finds a wide array of textures and light touch to be **overwhelming** to the nervous system. Light touch is easily misinterpreted as pain and can cause the nervous system to go into a state of fight or flight.

Students who are **under-responsive** to touch input are **not able to register** the touch cues that are required to function efficiently. For example, they do not notice that their clothes are twisted, that they have food all over their face or that they have messy hands.

BEHAVIOUR YOU MAY NOTICE

Students who are over-sensitive to touch may:

- throw their arms back when about to be picked up by an adult or pull away when you try to hold their hand (if they are young). These students' parents often say they never wanted to be held or cuddled as an infant. Students still may not accept cuddles or want to shake hands, unless they initiate this.
- become distressed when their nappies or pull-ups are being changed. They may well be equally distressed if they have soiled themselves, as the feeling on their skin may be unbearable.
- keep away from others to prevent accidental bumping or touching, which may mean they need greater personal space. It is quite common for them to dislike kisses and wipe the place where they have been kissed.
- avoid touching certain surfaces or textures, such as fabrics or carpets. Messy play may cause a fear reaction. Carpet time may be traumatic if a student's legs are not covered and the carpet is 'itchy'.
- prefer to touch or wear specific fabrics, which may often be soft in nature and well-worn. New, starchy clothes can be extremely distressing. Wearing an apron

for craft activities can also be uncomfortable, especially if it is plastic or has tight cuffs.

- not like to have their skin exposed, and so prefer to wear long-sleeved items (even if the weather is warm). Even a slight breeze or raindrop can be painful and distressing to these students. They might also prefer nakedness to clothes that do not fully cover them.

- request that all labels are removed from clothing and that no nametapes are sewn in. These students will often notice the seams on socks and where sleeves end. They may want to wear socks turned inside out to avoid ridges. Tight-waisted trousers can also be uncomfortable.

- overreact to minor cuts, scrapes, bumps and insect bites. They may have an extreme reaction to these incidents and be fearful of the scene of the incident for a long time afterwards.

- only use their fingertips, rather than the whole hand, to manipulate objects. They may also hold pens and paintbrushes far from the tip to avoid their hands being exposed to ink or paint. Following these activities, they will be very keen to wash their hands or wipe them on any available surface to remove 'mess'.

- avoid walking barefoot on grass or sand and be fearful of situations where they think they'll be expected to do this.

- find personal grooming extremely stressful – for example, getting haircuts, tooth-brushing and nail-cutting.

- react negatively or hit out when approached from behind. This is because the touch is unexpected, and their body has entered a protective fight-or-flight state.

- be excessively ticklish.

- sometimes be selective (or 'picky') eaters, only choosing to eat certain foods or textures. They tend to avoid mixing differently textured foods, as well as hot or cold foods. They may resist trying new foods.

- often have poor peer relationships as they are fearful of being touched, bumped into or being asked to take part in an activity they find uncomfortable.

● STRATEGIES FOR STUDENTS WHO ARE SENSITIVE TO TOUCH

Although students may be sensitive to light touch, deep-pressure touch can be soothing because it is 'tactile inhibitory'. Some forms of touch can be both: tickling is a good example of how light touch can be activating and arousing, as well as unpleasant at times. For those seeking touch, see **'The proprioceptive system'** below.

Soothing deep-pressure activities

- Firm massage (e.g. squeezing the arms or rubbing the back) or having a person press down on a student's shoulders – encourage older students to do this them-selves. See **'Self joint compressions'** in the **Photocopiable resources** section.

- A heavy blanket or weighted blanket on the student's lap, around their shoulders or something to lie beneath. Children must be supervised at all times by an adult for such activities. See information from individual manufacturers regarding correct weights and safety advice.

- Snuggling into a couch, under couch cushions or with cushions all around to form a 'nest'. You could have a large beanbag in the corner of the classroom for students to snuggle into.
- Weighted vests and squeeze vests. See information from individual manufacturers regarding correct weights and safety advice.
- A backpack (ideally weighing 10% of the student's body weight) worn for 20-minute periods. An adult can ask the student to put on their backpack during stressful times (e.g. during transitions).
- Asking the student to carry objects (e.g. books or shopping) for some time or over some distance. In order to manage this, it can be useful to have a book-swapping agreement with another teacher at the opposite end of the school!
- Using a 'steamroller' massage technique. This consists of rolling a large ball up and down a student's body while they lie on the floor, keeping the pressure firm.
- Using a 'person sandwich' massage technique. The student lies on and under cushions, pillows or beanbags to make a 'person sandwich'. You can then place deep pressure on their body, as if you were spreading the sandwich filling.
- Using a 'hot dog game' massage technique. The student lies on their stomach while you firmly rub their arms, legs and back. You then roll them up in a blanket or thin mat and, with one hand on their shoulder and one on their hip, rock them gently. You can also hum or sing with the rhythm of the movement.
- If a student is in residential accommodation, install a seat or bath board while they are showering or bathing. These help to reduce movement and allow the person to feel more 'grounded' and therefore calmer. This strategy can also be tried at home.

You can also work to avoid situations where there will be unexpected touch. Here are some suggestions.

- Place the student at the front or back of a line-up, rather than in the middle.
- Approach the student from the front to give a visual cue that a light touch is coming.
- Allow the student to have a larger personal 'bubble' than others. Use carpet squares or plastic hoops for floor-sitting as these will help to define each student's personal space.
- Use firm pressure to the shoulder or back, rather than a gentle hand placement or a brush to the sleeve, arm or face.

- Place the student's desk out of foot traffic and towards the edge of the room, so that the student has a good view of who is moving and where they are going.
- Try not to seat a left-handed student to the right of a right-handed student as bumping of elbows inevitably occurs!
- If acceptable, place a younger student on an adult's lap or next to a quiet student during a group gathering or carpet time. Place older students to the side or at the back of the group.
- Control the impulse to touch and do not take withdrawal personally.
- Warn the student ahead of time when they will be touched.
- Suggest that all new clothing is well-washed to make it as soft as possible. If you provide clothing in school, such as aprons or T-shirts, make sure these are suitable for students. Soft cotton aprons are preferable to stiff plastic ones, and large T-shirts may be better than tight-fitting ones.
- Lycra clothing under pyjamas and itchy uniform reduces sensitivities and provides calming pressure at the same time. Look for rugby skins, rash vests and sunsuits/tops – always in the sale at the end of the season!
- Allow students to wear gloves for art, food tech, etc.
- Choose soft fabrics for your school uniform and suggest that tags are cut off if students are very sensitive to them. Students could also wear seamless clothing. Easy-to-wear clothes with limited or no fastenings are best. Turning socks inside out to remove the ridge of the seam is also a good idea. Many large clothing brands are now producing easy-dressing ranges with no labels (information printed directly on to the garment), Velcro fastenings and elasticated trousers.
- Rather than sewn-on name tags, students' names could be written on their school clothes with a pen. Use undercover tape over any itchy stitching. Undercover tape is a commercially available adhesive tape that acts as a barrier between the skin and irritating seams or tags on clothing.
- Allow for deep-pressure oral stimulation by providing chewing gum, chewable jewellery or chewy tubes for this purpose.
- Use tangle spray and tangle brushes to reduce drag through hair. Brushes for use in the shower are also useful.
- Studies have shown that chewing gum is helpful for learning, and ideally this would be allowed by schools. If not, however, alternatives include straws, plastic tubing or the tops of sports bottles.
- Introduce aversive textures very slowly to build up tolerance. Use tools (e.g. a paintbrush) rather than fingers for painting.
- For hair cutting, try scissors with clipper attachments which make no noise or vibration. Use a weighted shoulder wrap under a gown for calming.

As well as the ideas mentioned above, the **Wilbarger Protocol** is a specific treatment technique that can be taught to parents or education staff by a trained therapist. It consists of methodical, deep brushing on the skin combined with joint compressions and can significantly help to reduce hypersensitivity. This intervention should only be used with full consent of the student and at their pace. If it is too uncomfortable, it should be stopped.

If you support students who crave touch, the following strategies may be helpful.

- Give students a variety of fidget toys to play with. Toys that can be squeezed or stretched are best (Blu Tack also works well). Let students choose their own fidget toy.
- Use weighted vests, lap pads or blankets.
- Play with Theraputty.
- Use a Theraband to pull and stretch.
- Engage in lots of messy play (see **'Messy play'** in the **Photocopiable resources** section).
- Define space for younger students. For example, they could sit in a hoop or on a designated area of carpet during group time to discourage them from constantly trying to touch their peers. Alternatively, they could sit on a wobble cushion on the floor, as this will provide movement.
- Try writing some Social Stories™ about personal space to share with students.

See **'The proprioceptive system'** chapter for further ideas.

THE GUSTATORY SYSTEM

The gustatory system is our sense of taste. Chemical receptors in the tongue, closely entwined with the olfactory (smell) system, provide us with information about different types of taste, such as sweet, sour, bitter, salty and spicy. Linked also to the tactile system, our mouth is able to determine the temperature, texture and movement of food or other objects in our oral cavity. At certain times, such as when we have a cold, foods can taste bland.

This can be an everyday experience for autistic students. It is important to mention Pica and ARFID here. Many autistic children have restricted diets and may be diagnosed with ARFID – avoidant and restrictive food intake disorder (DSM-5, American Psychiatric Association 2013).

Common causes for ARFID are:

- communication differences and reduced opportunities or motivation to engage in social imitation
- a history of choking, causing a real fear around eating and mealtimes
- a reduced taste and texture range and sensitivities around this
- fear/anxiety around anything new/unfamiliar (neophobia)
- poor self-regulation
- medical challenges such as constipation and acid reflux.

Pica can be described as 'eating items that are not typically thought of as food and that do not contain significant nutritional value, such as hair, dirt' (National Eating Disorders Association 2021). This can be associated with oral motor sensory-seeking compulsions, vitamin/mineral deficiencies and other mental health diagnoses.

Professional advice should be sought if you suspect a student displays AFRID and/or Pica.

An autistic student once said:

> Imagine that no matter what food you eat, whether it's your favourite meal or favourite dessert, that it all tastes the same – like bland, unsalted, unflavoured oatmeal or cream of wheat.

Students with sensitivity to certain foods or textures have often had negative experiences with food, such as gagging. Food is a very emotive issue for parents and carers, as to feed a child is to meet one of their most basic needs. Issues in this area need to be dealt with using great sensitivity and an understanding of students' underlying fears. You may need to consult a dietician to make sure that a student with a very restricted diet is consuming the correct vitamins and minerals.

● GUSTATORY (ORAL) HYPERSENSITIVITY

Students with gustatory hypersensitivity may:

- gag easily, sometimes even at the mere thought of certain foods. Students with a history of gagging will often be extremely fearful of food.
- prefer not to mix different food textures, such as liquids and solids. These might include yoghurt with fruit pieces or Bolognese sauce. If you offer these foods, they may simply be refused.
- have difficulty with certain textures and temperatures.
- appear to be fussy eaters because they will not eat certain foods based on texture, temperature, taste or smell. Their diet is often referred to as 'beige' as the foods they will accept tend to be this colour.
- not like having objects, such as toothbrushes, in their oral cavity. As a result of this, visits to the dentist can be difficult.
- show extreme distress before and during mealtimes. This is purely in anticipation of an activity that they find uncomfortable.
- need to control the mealtime experience and may only want to experience certain food textures, and use particular spoons, plates and cups.
- refuse to lick envelopes, stamps or stickers because they object to the taste.
- dislike or complain about the taste of toothpaste and mouthwash, and therefore avoid brushing their teeth. This can start a vicious circle of more serious dental treatment being required because teeth haven't been brushed.

● GUSTATORY (ORAL) HYPOSENSITIVITY

Students with gustatory hyposensitivity may:

- constantly put objects, fingers or food in their mouth. They may chew clothing, hair and fingers.
- overstuff their mouth at mealtimes because they do not feel when their mouth is full, or because they like the feeling of their mouth being stretched.
- prefer to eat extreme-tasting foods, such as lemons and hot sauces. In order for them to register the taste at all, it needs to be very strong. Many students never seem able to get enough condiments or seasoning on their food.
- lick, taste or smell everything, even non-food stuffs, to gain the sensation they require.
- drool excessively when past the teething stage, which may be a sign of under-sensitivity. It is also indicative of low muscle tone.
- love vibrating toothbrushes and even enjoy trips to the dentist!

● STRATEGIES FOR 'PICKY' EATERS WITH GUSTATORY HYPERSENSITIVITY

Above all, try to remain calm throughout the meal and keep arousal levels low. Otherwise, here are some strategies you can try at particular points during mealtimes.

Before eating, a student could:

- get used to oral stimulation by exploring their favourite toys orally. You could dip the toys into flavoured water, puréed foods, etc.
- play with their food. If they tend to throw their food, encourage them to put it into an 'all done bowl' instead. Always offer them the food you are eating so they can explore it. Discuss it with them by describing it – for example, by saying 'it's soft and green'. Food play is an excellent way to reduce the fear of food. See **'Food play activities'** in the **Photocopiable resources** section.
- listen to calming background music during meals, or have an alternative place to spend mealtimes away from the smells and noise of the dining hall.
- adopt good posture. Make sure students are sitting up properly and feel secure with their feet flat on the floor.
- benefit from soothing deep pressure or firm touch prior to and during mealtimes. This is because students who are hypersensitive to taste can also have touch hypersensitivities.
- use ankle weights to provide calming heavy work on the way to the dining room.
- before eating, look at a picture book that shows oral exercises such as 'how to warm up your mouth before eating'.
- use visual supports to show students what is for lunch. Allow a choice of food where possible, and also show them what will happen after lunch so they realise that mealtime will end!

During eating, you could:

- avoid presenting all foods at once. Instead, present them one at a time and on separate plates if necessary. This can stop students feeling overwhelmed. Sectioned plates are great for separating food without using three plates!
- consider cutlery choice. Some students simply hate the feel of metal cutlery in their mouth. Try plastic or horn cutlery.
- sit and eat as a family/group to introduce structure and routine.
- clear food away from the table when students indicate that they are done, before going on to the next type of food.
- pay attention to food temperature. In general, room-temperature foods are preferable.
- pay attention to food textures. When switching or changing foods, do so gradually. Consider mixing one food with the other by degrees until you have moved from the starting food to the target food.

SENSORY AND MOTOR STRATEGIES

- allow eating of preferred foods if there is a concern over restricted intake (in conjunction with professional advice).
- consider the noise in the dining hall. Allow ear defenders if necessary, place felt pads on table or chair legs and allow students who are hypersensitive to leave the room if it becomes too overwhelming.
- use heavy vinyl tablecloths that dampen the noise of cutlery on the table.

After eating, you could:

- give lots of praise for whatever successes students have had, even if they did not eat very much.

STRATEGIES FOR GUSTATORY HYPOSENSITIVITY

- Encourage students to chew 'mouth fidgets' such as gum or a straw.
- Encourage students to take part in oral motor games such as blowing bubbles or using whistles and vibrating toys. This may help to 'warm up' the mouth before meals.
- Crunchy foods such as pretzels and crackers and bread sticks are good at satisfying cravings for oral input.
- To reduce chewing on inappropriate objects, provide 'chews' such as chewy tubes, pencil toppers or pendants and bracelets designed specifically for this purpose. Have these available at all times.

THE AUDITORY SYSTEM

Our auditory (sound) system, or sense of hearing, allows us to hear someone talking to us, be aware of possible dangers and enjoy our favourite music and sounds. From an evolutionary point of view, the auditory system is one of our oldest. It is highly discriminative and links very closely to our vestibular system. The auditory nerves travel with the vestibular nerves to deliver information to the centres of the brain that deal with 'integration'. The intensity of sounds can also have an effect on our rhythm of body movement, either alerting or calming us, depending on the frequency.

Sensory processing differences in the auditory system manifest themselves in many different ways. You may have a student who cannot stand loud sounds, who covers their ears when they hear the vacuum cleaner, runs out of the toilets if hand dryers are activated or becomes upset when you try to sing to them. This is **auditory defensiveness**. These students experience most sounds as too loud, which can elicit a pain response.

The author Temple Grandin (1991) described over-sensitive hearing like this:

> My hearing is like having a hearing aid with the volume control stuck on super loud. It is impossible for an autistic student to concentrate in a classroom if he is bombarded with noises that blast through his brain like a jet engine.

Furthermore, the author Donna Williams described her experiences with sound as:

> I hear sounds that you cannot hear and sometimes it drives me crazy, people doodling with pencils and pens, shuffling chairs. I even hear the sound of air moving in the room, even the floor makes noise. Rain sounds like guns going off. Sounds in the same room are jumbled together. (cited in Boucher 2022, p.40)

In *The Sound of a Miracle* (1991), the writer Anabelle Stehli described how her daughter's hyper-acute hearing affected her sleep. She stated that at night she could hear her own body functions: the sound of her heart beating and the blood running in her veins. The constant noise from her own body was, to her, a terrible distraction that was often the cause of sleep deprivation.

If you have a student who mixes up words or misses important information, especially in noisy environments, they may have **auditory processing differences**. We will look at strategies that you can use for auditory processing differences later in this chapter.

● HYPERSENSITIVITY TO SOUND (AUDITORY DEFENSIVENESS)

Students with hypersensitivity to sound may:

- be distracted by sounds that others do not normally notice, such as humming lights or refrigerators, fans, heaters, ticking clocks, noises outside or at the window, or overhead projectors. They may hear a loud sound, such as an emergency siren, coming from a few miles away.
- often be fearful of the sound of a flushing toilet (especially in public bathrooms), vacuum cleaners, hairdryers, squeaky shoes, dogs barking, babies crying, hand dryers – especially newer models. Students may therefore avoid these noises or places where they're likely to hear them, at all costs.
- be distracted by loud or unexpected sounds. They may not be able to focus due to the noise level, even if you do not think the noise level is that high.
- often be bothered or distracted by background sounds such as lawn mowers, construction work outside or insects on windows. They will not be able to concentrate on what is happening in the classroom while these noises persist.
- frequently ask people to be quiet or to stop making noise (e.g. talking or singing) or complain of people yelling when this is clearly not the case.
- demand that only one person talks at once at the dinner table.
- dislike the sound of windscreen wipers in the car or on the school minibus. Rain on the window can also be distressing.
- often hum or sing to themselves to block out unwanted noise. Their humming is perceived by them to be 'safe' as they have total control over it.
- run away from certain sounds, or cry and cover their ears, even if the sound does not seem loud to you.
- refuse to go to cinemas, shopping centres, swimming pools, music concerts and so on because these environments are loud, echoic and unpredictable.
- decide whether they like certain people by the sound or volume of their voice. Try to use soft, rhythmic tones when speaking to sound-sensitive students.

● HYPOSENSITIVITY TO SOUND

Someone with hyposensitivity to sound may:

- fail to respond to verbal prompts and often will not respond to verbal cues, or to their name being called.
- hum or sing to themselves and appear to make noise for noise's sake. For instance, they may crash around, bang on surfaces, hit walls and so on. They often prefer very loud music and love to have the TV on at full volume. They are craving noise and will satisfy their craving however they can!
- seem to have difficulty understanding or remembering what was said, as they may not have tuned in to the finer points of a conversation. They may also often need directions to be repeated and will ask 'What?' frequently, even if you feel

they should have heard or that they had been listening. It also may take a few more seconds than average for these students to process information and to answer appropriately.

- appear oblivious to certain sounds that others react to and will often not be able to locate the direction of a sound, such as the siren on an approaching vehicle.
- often talk themselves through a task, aloud, and without realising this may distract others.

● STRATEGIES FOR STUDENTS WHO ARE SENSITIVE TO SOUND

- Give warnings ahead of time if you are approaching a place or situation where there will be more noise. Devices such as visual timetables or PECS (Picture Exchange Communication System) may be helpful. You may need to arrange for students to have a sanctuary space while out, such as a changing room or quiet corner. It may also be a good idea to take ear defenders or an MP3 player to mask noise, just in case. Consider offering white noise either through an app or a white noise machine.
- When sitting to work – at school or elsewhere – seat students away from sounds and noise if possible. Consider noise coming from outside as well as potentially subtle sounds within the classroom. For example, interactive whiteboards can hum and may be distracting. Students could benefit from white noise or soothing background music, possibly by using headphones and an MP3 player. For younger students, over-ear rather than in-ear headphones are recommended. It is also preferable to use a machine with a volume restrictor.
- Consider using a chatter tracker in class to 'police' the volume. The sensitivity can be altered depending on the activity. A great visual reminder for students and staff alike!
- Use calming strategies to help students better deal with any unexpected stimulation (see **'Calming activities'** in the **Photocopiable resources** section).
- Be aware that certain situations may be more of a trigger – for example, enclosed spaces such as gyms, cafés and school buses. It may be best to visit venues at quieter times. The venue should be able to advise you. Make sure you prepare students by using visual supports or even visiting the venue virtually first. Machinery such as vacuum cleaners, lawn mowers and hand dryers can also be an issue. Question whether it needs to be used when students are around.
- Carpeted classrooms, curtains and blinds minimise noise.
- Make use of quiet sanctuary areas at school. Dressing rooms or rest rooms provide good escape areas. You could also allow students a 'quiet space' where they can go if they feel they need it, or where you can ask them to go if they seem to be getting overwhelmed. Quiet areas could contain beanbags, cushions and duvets. Pop-up tents are great for younger students.

● STRATEGIES FOR STUDENTS WHO ARE UNDER-RESPONSIVE TO SOUND

- Allow students to listen to background music or background noise when needed, either through headphones or by switching on the television, radio or smart speaker. White noise can also be helpful – try using a fan or a white noise generator, which is a device designed specifically to make background noise.
- Help students to relax or sleep by providing background noise. You could try using a fan, a white noise generator or the radio.
- Students could use headphones if they are in a sanctuary area.
- It may be necessary to use auditory cues such as ringing a bell or clapping when you require a student's attention.
- Use visual cues such as traffic lights, chatter trackers or noise-o-meters to help students communicate a desired sound or noise level.

● STRATEGIES FOR STUDENTS WITH AUDITORY PROCESSING DIFFERENCES

- Reduce background noise at home and at school.
- Make sure that students are looking at you when you are speaking if this is not too uncomfortable for them.
- Speak at a slightly slower rate and at a mildly increased volume. Reduce language/spoken demands especially at times of increased stress.
- Always ask students to repeat the instructions back to you and to keep repeating them aloud (to you or to themselves) until the instructions are completed. It may also help to have a visual prompt, such as an object of reference or whiteboard showing the instructions.
- Allow students extra time to process information before you expect an answer. Remember, we all have differing processing speeds (like computers!) and this will also differ depending on our mood, stress levels and environment.
- Provide a quiet workstation with limited distractions (in terms of both materials and people).
- The use of ear defenders/calming ear plugs while working may limit potentially confusing auditory input.
- Environmental modifications such as classroom acoustics, desk placement and seating may help. Seek advice from an audiologist who can suggest ways to improve the listening environment.
- Download the Therapeutic Listening app and use the 'Quickshift' tracks to target sensitivity, discrimination, anxiety regulation and motor control. Note: This should not be used for students with epilepsy and professional guidance is recommended.

THE OLFACTORY SYSTEM

The olfactory (smell) and gustatory (taste) systems are closely linked. For instance, if you hold your nose, your sense of taste will be impaired. When we catch a cold, foods can taste bland.

Information from the receptors in our nose travels to the primitive brain structures that govern emotions, behaviour and memory storage, and to the brain's cortex, or outer layer, where conscious thought occurs. These links in the brain explain how odours can affect our thoughts, emotions and behaviour. Odours are used to detect danger (e.g. poisons), for pleasure and to help us navigate our environment.

Smell can be used to create a therapeutic environment that will facilitate improved functioning. Some students may become overactive when exposed to strong smells in the classroom, perhaps from a science lesson, a cooking activity or from people's perfume. Lunchtimes may also be challenging. Smell can be used to manipulate the environment (see the section **'Aromatherapy in the classroom'**).

Many students are sensitive to smells but some will actively seek out the smells they crave. Students may be compelled to seek out certain odours such as armpit smells and shampoos. Rather than taking this away from them, try to introduce 'sniff time' at regular intervals during the day using a scent on a handkerchief or smelly sticker, etc. This can help to manage anxiety and help calm.

In her book *Autism: Handle with Care!* (1995, p.60), Gail Gillingham describes her daughter's sensory sensitivities:

'You liked the smell of certain foods, and hated the smell of others, Georgie, but what about people? And animals?'

'I still have trouble with that,' she said. 'Dogs and cats and smells like deodorant and after-shave lotion. They smell so strong to me I can't stand it, and perfume drives me nuts.'

HYPERSENSITIVITY TO SMELL

Students who are hypersensitive to smell may:

- say 'You stink!' to staff who are wearing strong perfume or deodorant, or who perhaps ate strong-smelling foods at lunch. You may think that the shower gel, lotions and potions you used that morning were lovely, but these students will find them overpowering and they may make them feel sick.

- dislike or react negatively to smells that do not usually bother or get noticed by others, such as hand cream, shampoo, shoe polish or pen ink.
- refuse to eat certain foods because of their smell. They may smell food before eating and/or refuse to eat in certain rooms because of the way it smells.
- be seen breathing through their mouth instead of their nose.
- not visit certain environments such as farms, zoos or fish stores. Alternatively, they may bolt from these environments once there.
- not use the toilet at school due to the smell.
- often be distressed by household or cooking smells, even those that we perceive to be pleasant, such as freshly baked cakes. They may refuse to visit someone's house because of the way it smells.

● HYPOSENSITIVITY TO SMELL

Students who are hyposensitive to smell may:

- smell everything they touch to become orientated and comfortable with the object or thing. This could include touching classmates and staff.
- not notice noxious smells or discriminate between unpleasant and pleasant odours. They may not notice odours that others usually complain about such as manure spread in fields.
- actively seek strong odours, even smells such as urine or faeces. They may also wear strong-smelling perfumes and deodorants.
- often report that all foods taste the same and crave spicy, strong-tasting foods.

● STRATEGIES FOR HYPER-/HYPO-RESPONSIVENESS

- Try to limit exposure to smells; help students to be aware of strategies to help them avoid smells that they find unpleasant.
- Some students may crave certain smells that they perceive to be calming, such as their mum's shampoo. Rather than a student smelling many people to try to find this smell, place some of the desired smell on a sweatband or flannel.
- Ask if adults who work with these students can refrain from using strong perfume, hand cream, deodorant and so on in school.
- Introduce smells in a fun environment – make smelly play dough, cook with different essences, massage with smelly lotions, play with 'scratch-and-sniff' stickers. Work at the students' pace and allow them to leave if they become overpowered.
- If students have aversions to certain smells, it may be helpful for them to carry around a pleasant smell (in a small container with a hole in the top or on a handkerchief or sweatband) to use when bombarded with the smells they cannot handle.

- Use calming smells, such as those recommended in the **'Aromatherapy in the classroom'** section below.
- Provide healthy methods of stimulation, such as incense, scented candles, perfumes and aromatherapy (see below).
- Run regular activities that have a strong smell component, such as working with smelly play dough, playing in freshly cut grass or cooking with strong smells.
- Place a drop of scent on a sweatband for a student to smell at regular intervals. Use fragranced pulse-point roll-ons or scented nasal inhalers.
- Use 'scratch-and-sniff' stickers for students who crave smells that you find to be unpleasant. It is actually possible to purchase stickers which smell of faeces and rotting rubbish! Timetable these for use at appropriate times; it may prevent a student attempting to smell or smear their own faeces.
- For students craving smells, scented stationery and key rings are a useful addition to their school bag.

● AROMATHERAPY IN THE CLASSROOM
Methods of application

Massage: Essential oil must always be diluted in carrier oil. The safe dilution ratio for children is two drops of oil to 5ml of carrier oil.

Vaporisers: Four drops of oil in a burner or vaporiser. Do not let the burner run dry.

Footbath: Mix three drops of essential oil in 3ml of carrier oil and add to a footbath. Washing-up bowls with warm water are a good alternative for the classroom. Add marbles to the bowl for students to roll their feet over like a foot massage.

Sprays: Mix a few drops of essential oil in alcohol and top up with mineral water in a spray bottle. These can be used as room fresheners or to add a calming or alerting scent to the air.

Carrier oils

Carrier oils perform a variety of functions in aromatherapy. They are used to dilute the essential oils and contain vitamins and minerals, which may be of benefit and act as an emollient on the skin. They are beneficial to the skin as they nourish and balance the effect of the essential oil selected.

It is not advisable to use refined carrier oils from the supermarket as these may have been bleached and many of the vitamins and nourishing elements replaced with antioxidants and other additives to prevent cloudiness and increase shelf life.

Sweet almond oil: This is safe even for babies. It is a good emollient and has anti-inflammatory properties beneficial to students with skin problems such as eczema. Be careful not to use with students with nut allergies.

Grape seed oil: This is drying, so can be good for oily and spotty skin.

Evening primrose oil: This oil is an effective emollient and so very good for dry, scaly skin.

Sunflower oil: Only use cold-pressed, as allergic reactions can occur by using supermarket oil. It has softening and moisturising properties.

Starflower oil: This also has softening and moisturising properties.

Essential oils

For stress: Lavender, lemon, camomile, sandalwood (but not if students have a history of depression), grapefruit.

For anxiety and concentration: Rosemary (not to be used for students with epilepsy), mandarin and cedarwood, patchouli, neroli (not to be used for students with epilepsy), lemon.

For depression: Geranium, jasmine, bergamot and melissa, grapefruit, mandarin or tangerine.

For panic attacks: Ylang ylang.

Calming: Lavender, neroli (not to be used for students with epilepsy), ylang ylang, camomile, frankincense, mandarin or tangerine.

Uplifting: Rosewood, ginger, grapefruit or bergamot.

Oils in pregnancy

If staff or parents are pregnant, do not use basil, clarysage, cypress, fennel, jasmine, juniper, marjoram, myrrh, peppermint, rose, rosemary, sage or thyme. Safe oils are camomile, lavender, ylang ylang and tangerine.

Important note

If you wish to mix or blend essential oils, be sure not to exceed the amount stated in the 'Methods of application' section above. If you have any concerns, it is advisable to contact a qualified aromatherapist.

THE VISUAL SYSTEM

Sensory processing differences that affect the visual system may manifest in a number of ways. Students may exhibit visual defensiveness where they shield their eyes from bright light. There may be various processing differences that make reading or other activities more difficult. Students who become overly frustrated and angry when attempting to find things within competing backgrounds may have difficulties with visual perceptual abilities. These are all examples of difficulties with visual processing.

The author Donna Williams described her visual experiences before and after treatment with special coloured lenses (O'Mahony 2015):

> I saw my world in bits, so I got the ears of the cat, lost the head. Got the head and lost the body... When you use tinted lenses, you are filtering out an amount of incoming visual information (which) leaves your brain more time to catch up and to process what's left.

In her book *Sensing the City*, Sandra Beale-Ellis describes: 'I see everything in detail, but putting it all together into a holistic picture can often lead to sensory overload' (2017, p.23).

Difficulties with visual perception of depth are commonly reported among people with visual sensitivities. Navigating stairs and kerbs can be problematic, and people often say they need to watch their feet in order to walk properly. This can cause them to accidentally bump into objects and others.

Many autistic adults who experience these difficulties comment that faces and items 'pixelate' the longer they stare at them. This, along with visual discomfort, is often cited as the reason for reduced eye contact.

If you think that a student has visual sensitivity, it is suggested that they receive an eye examination by a developmental or behavioural optometrist.

BEHAVIOUR YOU MAY NOTICE

Students with sensory processing differences affecting the visual system may:

- stare at spinning objects for prolonged periods. They often appear to be lost in the moment.
- spin their own bodies in order to gain increased visual feedback.

- need to turn to face the opposite direction to their teacher when the latter is talking. This may be in order to listen, as the visual picture is too distracting.
- demand to wear sunglasses indoors. They may withdraw from any light source and want to keep blinds closed at all times.
- have desks or rooms that are extremely organised, meaning they know when an object has been slightly moved.
- complain of seeing double or distorted images.
- frequently lose their place when reading and/or copying from the board.
- give no eye contact or look beyond a person's face. If asked to give eye contact, they may not be able to focus on the task/question being asked of them, as it may be extremely uncomfortable for them to do so.
- miss visual clues and rely heavily on auditory prompts.
- have trouble locating a desired toy on a cluttered shelf due to experiencing visual overload. Equally, they may find it difficult to locate an object against a cluttered background, such as a pencil in a jumbled pencil case.
- turn or tilt their head when reading across a page to block out the glare or to see the print in a different way.
- frequently misjudge spatial relationships and bump into people or things.

● STRATEGIES TO HELP VISUALLY UNDER-STIMULATED STUDENTS

- Increase visual stimulation when teaching and playing. Use lots of hand gestures and extra visual supports such as hand puppets. You can also try bright lights and lots of colour and movement. Highlight text or use different coloured papers or headings.
- Alternate text colours per line.
- Use natural lighting or bright lighting.
- Add different visual components to tasks – for example, clapping or jumping when teaching maths, bright colours for teaching tools, use of film or video.

● STRATEGIES TO HELP VISUALLY OVER-STIMULATED STUDENTS

- Never force eye contact. It can be painful, uncomfortable and will not increase students' focus.
- It is important to minimise visual stimulation for students who are overwhelmed and/or give them a sanctuary space to retreat to.
- Encourage students to rest their eyes by closing them for 60 seconds regularly throughout the day.
- Teach students to only put the things they need for a task on their desk. This helps to reduce visual clutter.
- For those students with visual over-stimulation to light intensity or frequency,

use natural lighting whenever possible (but place students away from windows because they may be sensitive to direct sunlight).

- Use clear pencil cases so that it is easier to find objects.
- Consider having students assessed for coloured lenses (by a qualified professional).
- Allow them to cup their hands around their eyes to block peripheral vision. Wearing a peaked cap can also limit the intensity of light.
- Consider background colour on computers. This is easily changed via settings. Also, consider font.
- Try to avoid artificial, fluorescent lighting whenever possible. In addition to light-related considerations, many fluorescent lights produce a distracting humming sound that can affect or distract some students.

THE VESTIBULAR SYSTEM

Our vestibular system is responsible for detecting movement and how our body reacts against gravity. The vestibular system receives information when our head moves. It provides us with our sense of balance, orientates us within our environment and affects many skills including:

- 'gross' or large body movements such as walking, sitting, running and other activities
- 'fine' or smaller body movements such as writing, using forks and spoons, tying shoelaces or buttoning a shirt.

The receptors for our vestibular system are located within our inner ears. The semi-circular canals register movement of our head in any direction.

The utricle and saccule register changes in gravity as we move. This results in our perception of weight; we feel heavier if we move rapidly upward or feel lighter if we move rapidly downward (think about what it feels like on a playground swing).

The vestibular system influences all our other sensory systems. It is the unifying system in our brain that modifies and coordinates information received from other systems.

Muscle tone can also be influenced by the vestibular system. Muscle tone is necessary for good stability and balance, and differences in this area can contribute to difficulties in fine, gross and oral motor coordination.

Our vestibular system also plays a role in our attention and focus. For example, if you have been exercising, you will be more alert and focused. This is because of the extra vestibular input your brain has received from the movement. If you have spent the entire day seated or being very sedentary, you are more likely to feel a bit more sluggish and drowsy.

The vestibular system also supports the development of bilateral coordination, which is the ability to use both sides of our bodies in a coordinated manner.

Movement can have both a stimulating and a calming effect on our body. It can be easily overloaded, and we all experience differing levels of vestibular tolerance throughout our development. Many of us will know what it feels like to stimulate our vestibular system by riding on a spinning fairground ride. Some of us will leave the ride feeling sick and dizzy; others will immediately re-join the queue to ride again.

Students who feel sick are hypersensitive to movement and those who crave more movement are considered to be hyposensitive.

● BEHAVIOUR YOU MAY NOTICE

Students who have vestibular sensitivities may:

- seem to be thrill seekers, jumping from high places or climbing along the top of playground equipment. They often have no sense of danger and may encourage others to join them! Some may crave or avoid certain fairground rides, such as waltzers.
- enjoy spinning and never seem to become dizzy. Others love playground swings. They will swing very high and fast at every opportunity.
- if hypersensitive, be sedentary, cautious and hesitant to take risks, and will avoid movement. They may be fearful of movement, heights and of their feet leaving the ground, even when sitting if their feet are not supported. This is called gravitational insecurity.
- appear to be clumsy and/or have poor balance. They frequently trip, stumble and fall. They have difficulty changing direction and, if asked to take a different direction, may fall over. Hypersensitive students may become easily disorientated after bending over or turning around quickly.
- prefer lying down to sitting upright, as they feel safer in this position. They may constantly lean their head on their hand or arm, rather than sitting up straight.
- suffer from motion sickness when riding in a car, on a boat, on a train, on an aeroplane, on an escalator or in a lift. They may find that balancing when in these situations is very challenging.
- enjoy being upside down if hyposensitive. They will find every opportunity to fall without regard for their own safety or that of others. You may also notice that they have trouble staying seated. They need movement to maintain alertness and focus. They may rock unconsciously.
- easily lose their balance when riding a bike or climbing stairs, but this may not put them off trying and they may enjoy the thrill of falling if they are hyposensitive. If they are hypersensitive, they will avoid these activities altogether.

● STRATEGIES FOR STUDENTS WHO ARE HYPERSENSITIVE TO MOVEMENT

- Limit unnecessary movement where possible. Allow students to hold on during balancing activities and make sure they are seated in the classroom with their feet firmly on the ground.
- Consider small changes such as taking the stairs rather than using escalators.
- It is important to slowly introduce different movements in a safe way. Let students dictate the pace and make sure they feel safe by making use of mats or making sure there is someone for them to hold on to.
- Offer alternative activities for PE such as gym work which has less tumbling, running and jumping.

- Teach self-regulation strategies that students can use themselves to stay calm. Use proprioceptive activities to calm (see **'Proprioception – younger students'** and **'Proprioception – older students'** in the **Photocopiable resources** section).

● STRATEGIES FOR STUDENTS WHO SEEK INCREASED VESTIBULAR INPUT

- Give students the opportunity to move as much as possible by allowing them toilet breaks, giving them running errands, asking them to fetch things or to be a messenger, or by letting them clean the whiteboard (see **'Movement break ideas'** in the **Photocopiable resources** section).
- Alternate desk-based activities with 'movement' activities. Try thinking activities for 10–20 minutes, followed by movement such as bouncing on a therapy ball for 2–5 minutes, or different types of physical movement such as jumping jacks, squeezing stress balls or doing push-ups against a wall.
- Let students stand up and wiggle around whenever possible.
- Allow students to switch seats or move on/off a wobble cushion, as long as it is not too distracting for classmates.
- Use outdoor gyms.
- Consider the use of dynamic seating which gives hyperactive students an opportunity to move and provides them with sufficient stimulation in order to stay focused. Examples include wobble cushions, ball chairs and wobble stools.

THE PROPRIOCEPTIVE SYSTEM

The proprioceptive sense is our positioning sense. It allows us to know where our body parts are without looking at them. It is our sense of body awareness.

This sense underlies a person's ability to place body parts in a position in space and to 'grade' movements (judge the direction and pressure of a force) at an unconscious level. Proprioception aids motor planning and coordinating movements, emotional security and confidence.

If a child or young person with poor proprioception is asked to sit or stand still, they may well fall over. We have all experienced the loss of proprioception – for example, when our arm 'falls asleep' after we've leant on it. This can be distressing initially because we lose the sense that our arm is connected to our body. We may still be able to move the arm, but not in a coordinated way. When this happens, we also lose the sensory input from our muscles that tells us what we are doing.

Without proprioception, drivers would be unable to keep their eyes on the road while driving, as they would need to pay attention to the position of their arms and legs while working the pedals and steering wheel. We would not be able to type or play an instrument without staring at our fingers. We would be unable to put food into our mouths without the use of a mirror to help guide our hand to our mouth.

Our 'proprioceptors' are located within our muscles, joints, ligaments, tendons and connective tissues.

Every time that we contract, squeeze or stretch a muscle, or put weight on or stretch a joint, we stimulate the sensory receptors that tell us what our body is doing. This happens at an unconscious level in the brain. It initiates a process by which there can be an increase in certain neurotransmitters that enhance calmness, organisation and an increase in our ability to filter out extraneous sensory information. This is referred to as 'modulation'. If a person doesn't get feedback from their muscles and joints, and doesn't know what their body is doing or how to control it, it can be very frightening. Coordinating your body's movements becomes very difficult, challenging and tiring. Those who are not receiving input clearly from their proprioceptive system can find the world a stressful, challenging and frightening place.

Proprioception is closely linked with tactile and vestibular systems. Poor proprioception results in difficulties with interpreting body position and movement sensations.

The author Temple Grandin (1991) wrote:

> I craved deep-pressure stimulation. I used to get under the sofa cushions and have my sister sit on them. Pressure had a very calming and relaxing effect.

● BEHAVIOUR YOU MAY NOTICE

Students with poor proprioception may:

- pull, twist or chew on objects such as shirts, gum or pencils. This can interfere with concentration.
- frequently break toys or school equipment and/or hurt classmates unwittingly, as they do not have a clear understanding of their own strength.
- have difficulty with tasks requiring fine manipulation skills due to their heavy-handed approach.
- often lean on or bump into items or people, trip over or crash into objects.
- stamp their feet while walking to feel where they are going. They may kick their heels on chair legs, again to feel where their body is in space.
- often crave rough and tumble play to gain a feeling of their body in space.
- often prefer clothes and fastenings to be tight and like to be swaddled and wrapped in blankets. This helps them to feel where they are, and hence makes them feel safe.
- lack an awareness of body position in space and not seem to know what their own body is doing. They will rely heavily on their vision to check their movements.
- touch walls as they walk along, stay at the edge of an activity or at the perimeter of the playground. This gives these students the safety of touching something and feeling their way around.
- require movement to fire the proprioceptors in order to feel where they are in space. They may therefore rock back and forth on the floor and/or in a chair and fidget continuously. They need this movement in order to concentrate.
- often use too much pressure when writing – for instance, writing a letter repeatedly until they put a hole in the paper. This is because they are not gaining the kinaesthetic feedback to modulate the pressure.
- walk stiffly and appear uncoordinated and/or place their bodies in strange positions.
- crack their joints to gain sensory input.
- in extreme cases, resort to self-injurious behaviour to get the sensory input or feeling that is craved, either to feel less anxious or to feel where their bodies are.

● STRATEGIES FOR STUDENTS WITH POOR PROPRIOCEPTION

- Give students the opportunity to move as much as possible by allowing them toilet breaks, giving them errands, asking them to fetch things or to be a messenger, or by letting them clean the whiteboard.

- Alternate thinking activities with movement activities. Run desk-based activities for 10–20 minutes, followed by movement such as bouncing on a therapy ball for 2–5 minutes, or different types of physical movement such as jumping jacks, squeezing stress balls or doing push-ups against a wall.
- Let students stand up and wiggle around whenever possible. Provide non-distracting fidget toys such as putty, rubber bands, paperclip chains and squeeze balls.
- Allow students to switch seats.
- Place Therabands around chair legs, or commercially available bouncy bands for chairs, so that students can kick against them. Use commercially available leg or feet fidgets.
- Encourage students to do chair push-ups at regular intervals throughout the day.
- Consider the use of special seating which gives hyperactive students an opportunity to move and thus receive sufficient stimulation to stay focused. Examples include wobble cushions, ball chairs, hokki stools and fidget chairs.
- Keep water bottles at students' desks. Those with a sports top or straw work best. Chewing on a straw, a coffee stirrer stick or rubber tubing placed on the end of a pencil can all be helpful (make sure that plastic and rubber is free of the chemical BPA).
- With students on their tummies or backs, use a gym ball to do slow, rhythmical pushes back and forth. You could also make use of 'steamroller' massage techniques. With students lying down, roll a large gym ball up and down their body, keeping the pressure firm.
- Use a 'person sandwich' massage technique. The student lies on and under cushions, pillows or beanbags to make a 'person sandwich'.
- You can then place deep pressure on their body, as if you were spreading the sandwich filling.
- Try the 'hot dog' game. Have the student lie on their stomach, and then rub their arms, legs and back. Roll them up snugly in a blanket or thin mat. With one hand on the student's shoulder and the other on their hip, rock them gently.
- You could also hum or sing with the rhythm of the movement.
- Use therapy putty or modelling clay. Hide pegs in the putty and ask students to find them.
- Provide fidget toys such as pencil top fidgets, fidget cubes, Gripmaster hand strengthener or rough-sided Velcro dots on desks or rulers.
- Carry out deep-pressure (squeezing) activities. Start at the fingertips to shoulders and toes to thighs. Offer deep hugs (bear hugs) throughout the day.
- Wear tight clothing, Lycra clothing, wetsuits, etc. that give a little hug.
- Apply vibration or a massager to limbs, hands, feet and back. Do not apply to the neck, stomach or chest area.
- Squeeze sponges to transfer water from one container to another.
- Try blowing activities such as blowing bubbles through straws or blowing feathers.
- Go swimming.

- Do 20 wall pushes. Make sure that students are bending and straightening their elbows rather than moving their whole body. You can also do this with two students, both pushing against each other's hands or feet. For older students, try self joint compressions (see **'Self joint compressions'** in the **Photocopiable resources** section).
- Weighted items can be effective. These include weighted pencils, pens and cutlery, weighted blankets (make sure you follow safety guidelines as outlined by the manufacturer or prescribing therapist) and weighted vests. Try getting a student to wear a weighted vest for 20-minute periods (the vest should not be more than 10% of a person's body weight). Alternatives are weighted lap pads and wearing weights. You can also make neck wraps that are weighted to wrap over students' shoulders (fill a very long tube sock with large feed corn or beans). This could also be laid over a student's lap when they are sitting down.

For more strategies, see **'Proprioception – younger students'** and **'Proprioception – older students'** in the **Photocopiable resources** section.

THE INTEROCEPTIVE SYSTEM

Interoception is often known as the eighth sense. It is how we interpret sensations from our internal organs – for example, heart rate, hunger or needing to use the toilet. This is an area that is currently being researched and new theories are emerging.

Kelly Mahler (2021), author of the Interoception Curriculum, writes:

> At the most basic level, interoception allows us to answer the question, 'how do I feel?' in any given moment. Interoception also helps us control the way we feel, by prompting us to take action based on the signals we receive.

As with other sensory systems, the interoceptive system can be affected in individuals on the autism spectrum and/or with sensory processing differences. Research suggests that autistic participants seem to have significantly lower awareness of their interoceptive senses.

Sensations from our internal organs are detected through the nerve endings that line the respiratory and digestive tracts. They help us build a mental picture of the inside workings of our body.

Like the proprioceptive sense, interoception allows us to map out our internal feelings and helps us regulate our basic human needs such as hunger, thirst, respiration and bladder/bowel requirements.

The interoceptive sense also assists us to 'feel' our emotions. For example, before a fairground ride, your body may feel excited, your heartbeat may feel stronger and faster, your palms may become clammy, and you may feel butterflies in your tummy. These sensations help to identify that we feel excited; without them, we would have difficulty identifying our emotions and then reacting to them appropriately.

Interoception not only helps to identify emotions/internal sensations, but it is also critical for self-regulation. Interoception underpins our need to act. For example, to drink when we are thirsty, stop eating when we are full and go to the toilet when our bladder feels full.

Without these intuitive sensations, our bodies would become quite uncomfortable, but we may not know why.

As with all sensory systems, students can be hyper- or hyposensitive. Either way, they have difficulty interpreting their own body signals, which can lead to increased anxiety.

● OVER-RESPONSIVE

Students who are hypersensitive may find the internal workings of their body uncomfortable. They may be distracted, irritated or fearful of their own heartbeat. Some students may overeat to avoid the feeling of being hungry or be fearful of a bowel movement.

● UNDER-RESPONSIVE

Students who are under-responsive may not feel thirsty or hungry or feel when they need to go to the toilet. These students were often slow potty trainers and lacked motivation to feed as babies.

Some students seek to feel these sensations and will, for example, run around furiously to feel their heart pounding or withhold bowel or bladder movements as they enjoy the full feeling.

● STRATEGIES

- Always help students to focus on how their body is feeling. For example, clue them in by asking them to feel their breathing by placing their hand on their tummy, look in the mirror to see if they are flushed and feel their pulse rates. Use fitness bands with inbuilt heart-rate monitors to demonstrate increasing heart rate when anxious.
- An easy way to structure breathing is to use shapes to guide the breath in and out. Shape cards can be used and you can also teach children and young people to use objects in the home or classroom once they understand the technique, for example using the TV as the square or the edges of a book.

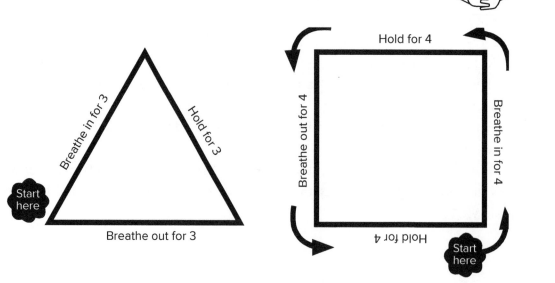

- Use proprioceptive and vestibular strategies to assist a calm alert state.
- Use listening therapy apps such as the Quickshift function on Therapeutic Listening. Choose tracks that target regulation.
- Yoga.
- Mindfulness activities.
- Relaxation incorporating deep breathing. Help them notice their heartbeat and the difference between excited and calm.
- Playing games and reading books related to emotions and feelings. As adults, we should ensure that we describe our emotions and inner feelings clearly – for example, 'My tummy hurts. I wonder if I am hungry?'
- Help students to recognise, identify and communicate feelings and emotions.
- Visualisation relaxation – bringing awareness and attention to the different parts of the body and referring to the sensations of breath, heartbeat, gurgling stomach, the weight of the limbs, etc.
- Movement activities can help a student become more aware and organised to understand their inner self.

Remember – fast, irregular and rotational movements are alerting, and slow, rhythmical and linear movements are calming. Discuss how this feels with students following the activity. Alert them to the inner feelings of their body such as heartbeat/rate, sweating, breathing rate, etc.

Having a student participate in movement before eating can help them be more alert and aid regulation. Again, remember that crunchy foods are alerting (pretzels, crisps, breadsticks, raw veggies) and chewy foods are calming (dried fruit, bagels, chewing gum).

- Using a reminder system (e.g. an alarm once an hour) can be helpful for children who are toilet training or need reminding to try.
- Schedule in consistent snack and toilet breaks.

MOTOR SKILLS STRATEGIES

MOTOR SKILLS OVERVIEW

R esearch and my clinical observations over the years have highlighted that many children on the autism spectrum and/or with sensory processing differences often have difficulties with posture, coordination and motor planning.

Research consistently shows that autistic children experience both gross and fine motor delays and/or atypical motor patterns (e.g. Green *et al.* 2002). A research study by Johnson-Ecker and Parham (2000) showed that children on the autism spectrum achieved lower scores in praxis tests than their typically developing peers.

Some children and young people have marked difficulties with gross (large) motor movements, which may manifest themselves as problems with balance (including balance required to sit), walking, running, riding a bike, throwing and catching.

Others are more affected at the level of fine motor skills. They may have trouble with manipulating, grasping, threading and buttoning.

Handwriting is a complex skill that is affected by both fine and gross motor difficulties, along with visual perceptual difficulties. If a student has difficulties with motor coordination, then very often handwriting is never going to be a true representation of their cognitive ability and will definitely not be a fun activity!

There are many theories as to why these motor difficulties are so prevalent in students on the autism spectrum. Below are a few possibilities but these are purely that – possibilities.

- **Differences in brain wiring:** This affects ideation, sensory integration, motor learning, coordination and praxis.
- **Joint hypermobility/low muscle tone:** This affects core stability, postural stability, muscle strength and overall stamina.
- **Anxiety:** This can affect willingness to participate in challenging and novel tasks. It can lead to avoidance of activities and therefore a reduction in the acquisition of motor skills.

Over the next couple of chapters, each area of motor difficulty will be expanded on and strategies provided, supported by worksheets in the **Photocopiable resources** section.

GROSS MOTOR SKILLS
Difficulties in this area can affect stamina, core/postural stability, balance, coordination and body awareness/body scheme.

We are all aware that children in general are less active than in previous decades. For those who have social interaction, communication, sensory and motor coordination difficulties, there is often little motivation to engage in physical activities. This can then exacerbate the problem and lead to a sedentary lifestyle which can impact physical health, arousal levels and alertness.

General activities for gross motor skills

- **Trampoline:** This is an excellent piece of equipment which helps children develop muscle tone, balance and motor planning skills.
- **Swimming:** Not only does this promote coordination skills but it also offers calming proprioceptive input.
- **Playground equipment:** Give children plenty of opportunities to climb, run, slide and swing.
- **Twister:** This is a great game, which is commercially available, to help develop balance and body awareness.
- **Different types of balls:** Encourage children to play games with a variety of different balls. Remember, larger balls will be the best ones to start with.
- **Animal games:** Pretend to be different animals by walking around on all fours – squatting like a duck, jumping like a frog, standing on tiptoes like a giraffe.
- **Rope games:** There are many games you can play with a rope to help develop balance, muscle tone and coordination. Some examples include walking along the rope on the floor, jumping over it and side to side, skipping and tug of war.

● CORE/POSTURAL STABILITY
Sitting posture

Students at school are expected to sit for long stretches of time. Most teachers these days are adept at using a multisensory approach to learning to optimise levels of alertness. They utilise hands-on activities and have students moving and changing positions throughout the school day. However, there are times when students are required to sit at their desks, listen and write/draw. Poor core/postural stability will affect the length of time students are able to sit without, for example, leaning on the desk, leaning on their hands, slouching and/or lying on the desk. Sitting for long periods can be both uncomfortable and exhausting.

Strategies

Chair and desk height: In an ideal world, budgets would stretch to desks and chairs of varying heights in each classroom. However, there are simple strategies that can help.

- Prop some books or a box under the student's feet. Place on non-slip matting to aid stability.
- Strap a booster seat to the chair to add stability for younger children.
- Commercially available chair and desk raisers.

Alternative chairs

Chairs with arms aid stability, and curved backs can assist both comfort and stability.

Some students with poor postural control may find chairs with built-in movement more comfortable as they prevent the feeling of the joints seizing up. The added bonus of movement chairs is that they improve core stability and increase levels of alertness at the same time! Below are some examples:

ball chair   wobble stool   fidget chair   inflatable cushions

Core stability activities

To be effective, these activities need to be carried out three times a week.

Activities to target core stability include:

- Lying on stomach and propping up on elbows. Use a wedge to give extra support if this is uncomfortable.
- **'Scooter board activities'** in the **Photocopiable resources** section.
- Activities in high kneeling and half kneeling such as throwing and catching or drawing against a wall.

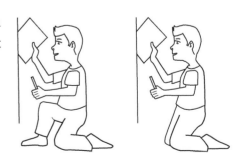

● BALANCE

Balance is closely linked to the vestibular and proprioceptive systems. Children must learn to balance before they can progress to higher-level motor skills. Without sufficient balance skills, it is difficult, for example, to put trousers on, ride a bike, sit while carrying out motor tasks such as writing, and climb and descend stairs.

Activities to improve balance and stability

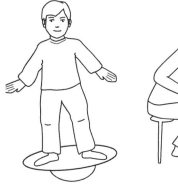

- Trampoline.
- Gym ball/space hopper activities (see **'Therapy gym ball activities'** in the **Photocopiable resources** section).
- Jumping, skipping, hopping.
- Outdoor play equipment such as swings, climbing frames, trim trails.
- Balance beams or upturned benches.
- Balance stools and balance boards.
- Stand on a wobble cushion. Try with one leg or two. Once this is easy, try catching and throwing games.

● BODY AWARENESS/SPATIAL AWARENESS

This refers to one's awareness of body parts or dimensions and is closely linked to our proprioceptive system. The development of spatial/body awareness helps us to understand the concepts of direction, distance and location.

Children who do not have adequate body awareness often appear clumsy or awkward. They frequently have difficulty with gross and fine motor activities as these activities require subtle changes in posture, strength, force or dexterity, such as judging the direction, force and speed of a ball coming towards you.

Body/spatial awareness is the foundation of coordination.

Body/spatial awareness activities

- Proprioceptive input (see **'Proprioception – younger students'** and **'Proprioception – older students'** in the **Photocopiable resources** section). This gives our muscles and joints information about how our arms, legs, head and trunk move and where they are in space. Any weight-bearing 'heavy work' activities are technically proprioceptive input – for example, star jumping, stomping the feet, push-ups, carrying heavy objects, weights and skipping.
- Therabands activities (see **'Proprioception – older students'** in the **Photocopiable resources** section).
- Commercially available games such as Twister.
- Simon Says.

- 2D and 3D puzzles.
- Brick designs/models. Copy a picture.
- Mirror games. Partner up with a peer. When one person moves, the other person copies their movements exactly. See the ideas on the chart below but have fun making up your own moves.

- Outdoor play equipment such as climbing frames and tunnels.
- Outdoor gyms.
- Animal walks.
- Swimming.
- Target games such as beanbags into hoops, buckets or a circle chalked on the playground.
- Obstacle courses. The ability to negotiate an obstacle course requires a significant amount of spatial awareness. Vary the courses and include activities that require going up, over, under and around objects.
- Maps. Follow a treasure map or, for older students, map-read to a point of interest.
- **'Infinity walk'** in the **Photocopiable resources** section.

OBJECTIVES OF YOGA SESSIONS

Autistic students with sensory processing differences often have elevated levels of anxiety, which can cause their bodies to become stuck in fight-or-flight mode. This in turn causes physiological changes in the body, causing the blood to divert from the digestive organs to the skeletal muscles. This results in disrupted digestion, increased heart rate and shallower breathing – all of which increase anxiety.

In 2012, researchers investigating the efficacy of the 'Get Ready to Learn' yoga programme among children with autism spectrum disorders found that 'use of daily classroom-wide yoga interventions have a significant impact on key classroom behaviors among children with ASD' (Koenig, Buckley-Reen and Garg 2012).

The main benefits

- Increased motor learning. Deficits or difficulty with motor coordination is often a common thread among children on the autism spectrum. Yoga helps to tone muscles, stretch ligaments and develop body awareness.
- Improving the communication between the left and right hemispheres of the brain using bilateral exercises.
- Improved balance and coordination.
- Improved core and trunk stability, including posture.
- Increased self-confidence and social interactions. Poor coordination often leads to low self-esteem as students are often singled out or teased for not excelling in sports or being clumsy. By learning self-control, motor control and self-calming techniques through yoga, confidence will increase. Learning to work together in a yoga class can also increase confidence and enhance social interactions within group settings.
- To enhance a calm and alert state in readiness to learn. Autistic students with sensory processing differences often suffer from a highly sensitive nervous system which is easily over-stimulated by the eight senses documented in the sensory sections of this book. Yoga's natural setting of dim lights, soft music and comfy mats creates a comforting environment with reduced external stimuli.

Yoga's physical poses allow nervous energy to be released from the body in a controlled manner and encourage a calming sensation.

All in all, yoga provides a toolbox for teachers, parents and students themselves. It is a transportable practice that can be used in a variety of environments with no equipment required.

CORE STABILITY

Autistic students and those with sensory processing differences often have difficulties with posture, coordination and motor planning. Core strength is central to everything we do and impacts on all areas of development. Poor posture is often caused by poor core strength, which results in gravity pulling down and can lead to hunched sitting, poor stamina when standing and weak arms, for example.

A stable core = a stable base. Poor core stability is closely linked to challenges in students' vestibular and proprioceptive systems, which relate to balance, coordination and body awareness.

Not only does core stability help fine and gross motor skills, but it plays a key role in emotional self-regulation and sensory processing. Students need to have calm control over their bodies to be able to focus and concentrate.

Students with poor core strength and stability usually present as clumsy and fidgety; they will slump over their desks and can seem to be under-aroused as they are tired from attempting to hold themselves in an upright position. Poor core stability also affects functional activities such as handwriting, walking, running and overall stamina.

Many students with sensory and motor challenges have difficulty effectively stabilising their core before they move or attempt activities requiring a stable base of support such as handwriting.

Along with the neck, shoulders, spine and pelvis, the diaphragm is another very important core muscle.

Therefore, it is essential for children and young people to breathe while carrying out core stability activities and not hold their breath.

Students with poor core muscle strength often present with other challenges such as toe walking (which also has a tactile and proprioceptive base) or sitting in the W-position (this is when a child sits on the floor, knees bent, feet positioned outside of their hips and their bottom on the floor), as these result from motor difficulties linked with sensory processing differences.

Although toe walking can result in shortened Achilles' tendons and other physiological changes, intervention should be approached with some caution as it also has many benefits. Williams *et al.* 2010 consider it in this way: 'Some studies conclude that children with differences in vestibular processing can also have tactile senses that exacerbate their toe walking. They may not like the feeling of the floor touching their feet, and toe walking minimizes this contact. Children seeking proprioceptive input toe walk, because the gait prolongs stimulation of joint receptors and causes their muscles to tighten. The movement provides a calming input sensation for the child.'

Key indicators of poor core stability

- When at a desk or table, rather than sitting upright, a tendency to slump all over the desk, propping the head in a hand or leaning on elbows.
- Hooking legs around chair legs or arms around the back of the chair for stability.
- Fidgeting on chair. Rocking back and forth.
- Constantly leaning against walls, people, etc. rather than standing upright. This is especially evident for prolonged standing.
- Preferring to lie down on the floor or sofa to watch TV instead of sitting upright.
- Difficulties with balance while lifting one leg off the ground (e.g. when putting on trousers).
- Losing balance easily during gross motor activities and sports. Clumsy, bumping into things.
- Sedentary play to avoid too much coordination.
- Lower back pain can be associated with a weak core strength.

Activities to strengthen the core need to be carried out regularly to be effective. See **'Core stability'** in the **Photocopiable resources** section for activity ideas. However, being involved in sports, gymnastics, swimming lessons, horse riding, trampolining, going to the swing park or outdoor gym will all help with balance, coordination and core strength.

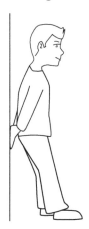

FINE MOTOR SKILLS

Developing fine motor skills is often a challenge for many autistic people. The combination of both sensory and motor skills together, along with following complex coordination patterns to perfect the activity – for example, cutting food with a knife and fork, buttoning a shirt or handwriting – can be extremely frustrating.

Efficient fine motor skills are underpinned by the following skills:

- balance
- eye motor control (this is the ability for our eyes to work together in order to follow and/or hold an object in the line of vision as needed)
- hand–eye coordination
- manual dexterity
- hand and finger strength
- body awareness (proprioception)
- bilateral coordination – using two hands together with one hand leading (e.g. cutting with scissors while holding the piece of paper)
- crossing midline – the ability to cross the imaginary line running from a student's nose to pelvis that divides the body into left and right sides
- hand dominance
- concentration/focus
- motivation!

To acquire these skills, the environment needs to be tailored to meet any sensory difficulties.

It is essential to establish adequate gross motor skills before moving on to tackling more complex fine motor activities. For example, children should have strength and dexterity in their hands and fingers before being asked to manipulate a pencil on paper. The larger joints of the body, such as the shoulder and pelvis, need to be stable before the hands can be free to work on specific skilled fine motor activities. If you are unable to balance on a chair without holding on, it's impossible to use a pencil at the same time!

Many activities will target more than one skill area. For example, scissor activities will exercise the same muscles needed to manipulate a pencil in a mature tripod grasp.

Children also need to develop hand dominance to have a clear 'helper and doer' hand. This assists bilateral (two-sided) activities such as cutting with scissors and using a knife and fork.

Repetition is the key to developing motor skills, and interventions should be regular and short in length to maintain engagement in the activity. Strategies to minimise sensory sensitivities also need to be considered – for example, wearing headphones to block out sounds, alternative seating to aid balance or provide movement, and using spongy pen grips (see the chapters about each sensory area).

Overall, activities should be fun and, where possible, be themed to the students' interests to maintain motivation and prevent resistance!

VISUAL MOTOR INTEGRATION

Visual motor integration is the coordination of visual perceptual abilities and fine motor control. It is a skill that allows our eyes and our hands to work together in a coordinated and efficient way.

Students who struggle to integrate/coordinate their visual systems and their motor systems may struggle with handwriting, copying, throwing and catching a ball as well as other school skills. Their handwriting may seem disjointed and lacking in fluency. Handwriting for these students will therefore require an increased amount of conscious effort that is out of proportion to the task, therefore leading to fatigue, frustration and decreased motivation.

COMPENSATORY STRATEGIES

- Colouring inside the lines. Drizzle PVA glue around the outlines of large colouring pictures to give a definitive and tactile edge. Use Wikki Stix or wool glued around the area to be coloured in.
- Difficulty stringing beads. Use pipe cleaners, wooden dowels or Sellotape at the end of the string to prevent wobbly string.
- Difficulty lining up maths equations or spacing words. Use graph paper or squared paper.
- Writing and drawing on a vertical or slanted surface improves viewing angle and hand/wrist position. Drawing can be done on an easel or even on paper taped to a wall. An angled writing board can be placed on a desktop for writing tasks.
- Lying on their tummy helps with developing shoulder stability and an upright head. This can be done for writing, drawing and play activities.
- Alternatives to writing by hand for students with significant challenges include learning computer skills, dictating to a scribe, voice recordings, having a peer note-taker or getting a copy of notes. It is important to teach and allow time for word-processing skills to improve so students can use computers effectively in place of handwritten assignments.
- Avoid visually complex worksheets. When worksheets cannot be modified, have students cover up all the problems except the one they are working on with a piece of paper to reduce overwhelming visual information.
- Allow the use of cursive or print on written assignments.

- Modify the assignments and materials when necessary by shortening assignments (striving for quality, not quantity).

● ACTIVITIES TO IMPROVE VISUAL MOTOR INTEGRATION

- Make shapes with sticks (toothpicks, lolly sticks, Wikki Stix, etc.). Ask students to copy design exactly using their sticks, toothpicks, etc.
- Have students use various materials (toothpicks, lolly sticks, Wikki Stix, etc.) to make their own shapes.
- Half-to-whole drawings. Draw half of a simple picture (pizza, house, person, tree) and students draw the other half.
- Lacing cards. Try unusual ways to lace around the edges.
- Beanbag toss games. Go for a target such as a container or bin – large at first and then smaller as skill improves.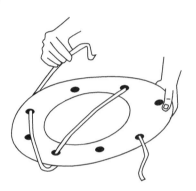
- Balloon volleyball. For added challenge, place a marble or penny inside the balloon – it will make the game more unpredictable.
- Hit a balloon with a tennis racket or paddle. Carry out standing up and/or lying on tummy using two hands.
- Rolling ball with two hands. Bowling by knocking over skittles or two-litre bottles.
- Tape a target to the wall and throw a ball. Decrease the size of the target over time.
- Torchlight tag. While lying on your back in a darkened room, play tag or follow the leader with your flashlight beams.
- Torchlight fun. Tape up 5–10 target items (i.e. coloured post-it notes) around room, turn out lights and use a torch to locate all targets.
- Obstacle courses.
- Copy block designs. Start with copying completed brick designs and move on to copying designs drawn on paper.
- Stringing beads. Copy bead patterns or create repeating patterns.
- Geoboards. Copy shapes and letters using rubber bands on geoboards.
- String colourful beads, macaroni or cereal hoops on to pipe cleaners, straws, etc.
- 'Speed Stacks' – a fun cup-stacking game (see **https://speedstacks.uk**).
- Games that encourage diagonal awareness help with drawing. These games include noughts and crosses and Connect 4.
- Body direction games such as Twister.
- Construct simple to more complex origami figures.
- Play torchlight tag by shining a torchlight on a wall and moving it up and down, left and right, and so on. Have students follow your pattern.
- Jigsaws.

- Simon Says – emphasise the right or left side.
- Skipping with rope.
- Line tracking games. Animated line tracking available on **www.eyecanlearn.com**.

VISUAL PERCEPTION

Visual perception is the ability to see and interpret – to give meaning to the visual information all around us. Visual perceptual skills are essential for us to make sense of what our eyes see. It is not about visual acuity – whether you have 20/20 vision – but more about how our brain processes the information it receives visually.

If our visual perception is inaccurate, incorrect or altered in any way, problems with reading, spelling, handwriting, cutting, dressing, maths and comprehension may occur.

Visual perception is often split between differing areas as below:

- **Visual discrimination:** the ability to determine differences or similarities in objects based on size, colour, shape, etc.
- **Visual figure ground:** the ability to locate something in a busy or cluttered background/environment.
- **Visual memory:** the ability to recall visual traits of a form or object. This can be long- or short-term memory.
- **Visual spatial:** understanding the relationships of objects within the environment. This includes your own body parts. It also involves being able to tell how far objects are from you and from each other.
- **Visual attention:** the ability to focus on important visual information and filter out unimportant background information.
- **Visual sequential memory:** the ability to recall a sequence of objects in the correct order.
- **Visual form constancy:** the ability to know that a form or shape is the same, even if it has been made smaller/larger or has been turned around.
- **Visual closure:** the ability to recognise a form or object when part of the picture is missing.

Students with visual perception difficulties may struggle with:

- finding items in a cluttered environment such as a pen in a bag or socks in a drawer
- completing puzzles or dot-to-dots
- spatial concepts such as in, out, on, under, next to, up, down, in front of
- differentiating between b, d, p, q and letter/number orientation
- keeping their place on a page when reading or writing
- remembering left and right

- judging the depth of steps and stairs
- sequencing letters or numbers in words or maths problems
- remembering the alphabet, days of the week, months of the year in sequence
- map reading, especially if the map is turned around
- copying words and pictures from one place to another (e.g. from whiteboard to paper, from book to paper)
- dressing (e.g. matching shoes or socks)
- discriminating between size of letters and objects
- remembering sight words
- detailed drawings
- completing partially drawn pictures or stencils
- filtering out visual distractions
- sorting and organising personal belongings
- navigating around buildings
- catching and throwing games
- hidden picture activities or finding a specific item in a cluttered desk or pencil case.

Difficulties with the above can often lead to frustration, avoidance, poor attention, exhaustion and loss of self-confidence. These students often benefit from a multisensory and kinaesthetic learning environment with the addition of using auditory skills to aid recall – for example, alphabet or periodic table songs.

● STRATEGIES

- Place students in the front row or in a designated work area with minimal visual distractions. If they are sitting at the back of the classroom, they may be distracted by stimuli all around.
- Encourage students to keep a tidy and uncluttered desk.
- Avoid too much detail on classroom walls. Use only relevant pictures or aids.
- When reading, use a book marker or coloured reading ruler below the sentence that is being read.
- Minimise the information presented on worksheets and enlarge worksheets to ease focus demands.
- Remove irrelevant information from the board if students are copying from it. Limit the amount of copying from the board. Use a document holder next to students to reduce distance from work to paper.
- Use a cut-out window to show one problem/question at a time.
- When projecting work on the whiteboard, use different colours for each line, use large print and have points clearly numbered.
- Underline sentences in different colours when copying work.
- Directional arrows to help with direction or starting position (e.g. for letter formation). Use direction arrows for letter formation and add verbal cues such as 'around, up and down for the letter d'.

- Graph paper to help with word spacing and sizing.
- Use highlighter pens to emphasise key facts.
- Highlight the outlines of pictures that need to be coloured in or cut out.
- Use assorted colours to indicate different mathematical symbols.
- Visual cues – for example, use a coloured dot or sticker to show what side of the page to start writing on or reading from, or place a mark or sticker on the inside of the child's shoes so they know which foot to put them on (place the dots on the inner rim of shoe and put shoes down so the dots are touching each other).
- Reinforce with verbalisation and movement. Give students spatial cues when looking for information – for example, 'Find the picture with the house at the top right-hand side of the page.'

● ACTIVITIES TO HELP IMPROVE VISUAL PERCEPTION

- Hidden picture games in books such as *Where's Wally?*
- Picture drawing. Practise completing partially drawn pictures.
- Dot-to-dot and maze worksheets or puzzles.
- Memory games. Playing games such as Memory.
- Sensory activities. Use pipe cleaners and Wikki Stix to form letters and shapes. Feel the shape with eyes closed to help students visualise the shape.
- Wordsearch puzzles that require you to look for a series of letters.
- Copy 3D block designs.
- Identify objects by touch. Place plastic letters into a bag and have students identify the letter by feel.
- Review work. Encourage students to identify mistakes in written material and correct them in a different colour to the text.
- Recall object or picture features. Let the student look at an object and talk about its features. Then take the object/picture away and ask them to recall some of its features/details.
- Kim's game. Place everyday objects on a table. Show them to the students for about a minute, then cover them and see how many each can recall. This can also be played by taking one object away and asking the students to identify the object that is missing.
- Identify which object is missing from one of two almost identical pictures. Spot the difference.
- Visual memory spelling games. Using the look, cover, remember, write, check strategy with simple high-frequency words.
- Give students a magazine page and ask them to circle all instances of the word 'the' or the letter 'a' in one minute or find all red objects, all squares, etc.
- Ask students to find an object within their surroundings such as a bird in a tree, or I-spy games.
- Find various categories of objects in the room, such as all the round objects or all the red objects.

- Carry out specific instructions that involve looking for and fetching things – a treasure hunt.
- Obstacle courses with 'in, out, over and under' activities.

HANDWRITING

Handwriting is needed for academic achievement and is used in many areas of daily living, such as signing a greetings card, writing an envelope or jotting down a message following a phone call.

Thankfully, improving technology has reduced the pressure on students struggling to represent their cognitive ability in written form. Laptops are becoming commonplace in many classrooms today, and the smartphone is also a fantastic tool to reduce the need for physically writing notes, lists and messages.

However, handwriting remains an important skill in many educational establishments, and students with sensory motor difficulties can find the acquisition of legible handwriting quite a challenge. Students who struggle to write often miss content while focusing on the mechanics of writing.

The acquisition of handwriting that is legible and fluent requires a firm foundation of motor skills.

A study to examine handwriting quality in children on the autism spectrum (Fuentes, Mostofsky and Bastian 2009) concluded that there is a relationship between fine motor control and poor quality of handwriting in autistic children.

The researchers found that the handwriting of autistic children was poorer than typically developing children. Specifically, autistic children had trouble with letter formation rather than the size and spacing of letters.

Handwriting difficulties are also closely linked with sensory processing differences, especially the tactile, proprioceptive and vestibular systems. These sensory systems are essential for the development of grasp patterns, fine motor manipulation, control and force on the pencil, balance and speed of movement, etc.

If handwriting is clearly causing huge amounts of anxiety and pain, then stop. Move on to technology and focus on improving keyboarding skills.

● PREREQUISITE SKILLS REQUIRED FOR HANDWRITING

Below are just a few prerequisites required for successful handwriting. It's no surprise that students with any sensory motor processing differences struggle!

- Body and spatial awareness.
- Lateral and bilateral coordination to be able to use two hands together effectively, one to hold the pencil and the other to stabilise the page.

- Visual perception, visual motor integration and form and space perception which are needed to recognise letters/words and position words on the paper.
- Postural stability. Without this, students may slump and lean on their desk, keep their heads close to the paper or sit on their feet for stability.
- In-hand manipulation skills, hand strength and dexterity.
- Eye–hand coordination.
- Sensory integration including adequate tactile information to feel the pencil, knowing how tightly to hold it, how hard to press, etc.
- Memory for letter formation, spelling and sequencing.
- Attention, focus and motivation.

● SEQUENCE OF HANDWRITING DEVELOPMENT

- Random scribbles/mark making on paper.
- Circular scribbles.
- Colouring.
- Basic shape formation.
- Letter formation.
- Printing words.
- Cursive words.

● PENCIL GRIP DEVELOPMENT

| Palmer/cylindrical grasp – movement mainly coming from the shoulder. | Pronate digital grasp – movement coming mainly from the shoulder and elbow. | Static tripod grasp – movement mainly from wrist. | Dynamic tripod grasp – movement to form letters coming mainly from the fingers. |

● PRE-WRITING SHAPES

- It is generally agreed that children should be able to replicate the shapes below before proceeding to formal letter formation.

● GENERAL TIPS FOR SUCCESS

- Posture – desk and seat height. Ensure a good base of support and a non-slippery surface on the chair. Feet need to be flat on the floor or on a box/book, not dangling, hips at 90 degrees, and the desk should be at the correct height.
- Paper position – paper should be angled to around 45 degrees (to the left for right-handers and to the right for left-handers) and placed away from the edge of the table. Tape some masking tape on the desk to remind students of where to position the paper.
- Upper body strength and postural control are essential. A student's neck, trunk and pelvis need to be stable to support the other limbs and prevent fatigue. See **'Core stability'** in the **Photocopiable resources** section.
- Angled writing surface – non-slip surface. This offers postural support and defines personal space.
- Ensure the paper does not slip if students do not effectively use their helper hand to do this. Use non-slip matting, bulldog clips or Blu Tack.
- Warm up to activate muscles to maintain good posture and grip – see **'Handwriting warm-up'** in the **Photocopiable resources** section.
- Hand and finger strength is important because writing is tiring. Poor finger and hand strength can discourage students from persevering. See **'Fine motor skills activities'** and **'Multisensory approach to handwriting'** in the **Photocopiable resources** section.
- Utilise pen grips. Trial a few different ones to find the one that works best. Thick triangular pencils and chalk are good starting points. Start with short pencils to aid control – either purchase these or simply cut a standard pencil in half.

Paper choice

- Buff-coloured paper reduces visual stress.
- When practising, use surfaces that provide extra kinaesthetic feedback such as chalkboards, sandpaper and textured wallpaper (free samples are readily available from large DIY stores).
- Colour-code the margins.
- Use squared paper to aid letter spacing.
- Try paper with different line spacing.
- Try paper with raised lines to increase feedback.
- Use 'spacers' to measure between words.

There are many ways to prepare students for writing, but it's important to remember all the prerequisite skills that underpin success. Using a multisensory approach along with lots of pencil practice is the key to students learning and retaining information. Engaging in multisensory activities while learning to write gives the brain additional opportunities to integrate and store the information so that it is available for the future.

SCISSOR SKILLS

●●●●●●●●●●●●●●●●●●●●●●●●●●●●●●

● PREREQUISITES FOR SKILLED SCISSOR USE

- Balance – ability to sit in an upright posture, with feet supported, to be able to freely use hands.
- Shoulder stability – this is needed to be able to reach forwards and upwards and provides support to the forearm, wrist and finger actions that are required for cutting.
- Forearm control – the ability to move forearms from a palm down (pronated) position to a thumb up (neutral) position is needed to guide the scissors.
- Grasp – a strong grasp is needed with the ability to open and release the hand automatically.
- Dominant and helper hand – ability to use two hands together, one for cutting and one to guide the paper/material being cut.
- Coordination of arm, hand and eye movements.
- Developmental readiness.

● WHAT SCISSORS TO USE?

Believe it or not, there are different types of scissors available to assist with learning to cut. It is important to try a few and find the pair that make the job the easiest. For left-handed students, it is essential to use left-handed scissors to ensure the cutting blade works efficiently.

Remember – during scissor practice, encourage students to cut with 'thumbs up'. They should not be holding their thumb toward the floor while cutting.

- Spring-loaded/self-opening scissors are great for students with poor motor control. They have a spring fitted to automatically reopen the scissors after each 'squeeze' to help with the motor control required.
- Double-loop training scissors have double loops on each handle allowing a teacher or parent and student to cut together. These are ideal for use by students with reduced grip strength.

- Easy grip/loop scissors are perfect for beginners or for students who have trouble opening and closing scissors. They are also ideal for students who have not yet established a hand dominance as they can be swapped between right- and left-hand use. They reduce the amount of coordination required, too.

- Cushion grip scissors. There are a variety of scissors on the market with cushioned and non-slip grips which may be more comfortable for a student with tactile sensitivities.

When first learning to cut, it is important to use the correct type of material. Firm paper can be much easier than thin flimsy paper that bends and moves while trying to cut.

It is also important to pitch the activity correctly to ensure success. Start with easy tasks such as snipping paper to make decoration/collages or snipping play dough snakes, and slowly progress to more complex shapes. As always…keep it fun!

● ACTIVITY IDEAS TO IMPROVE CUTTING SKILLS
See 'Bilateral coordination (using two hands)' in the Photocopiable resources section.

Pre-scissor skills
These activities work on the concept of opening and closing as you would with scissors.

- Use kitchen tongs and/or tweezers. Pick up various objects such as cotton balls, play dough, marshmallows, small blocks, etc. with the tongs or tweezers and drop into a cup. You could set up races to see who can fill a cup the fastest! There are also lots of commercially available games that use tongs/tweezers.
- Play with water guns, turkey basters, water bottles, spray bottles, squirt toys, etc. Squeeze and release to make water come out. You can do this outdoors by painting the pavement, walls, paving stones, etc. (or put food colouring in the water and paint the snow).
- As a tabletop activity, use medicine droppers filled with water and drop on to blobs of felt tip drawn on blotting paper/coffee filter. Watch the colours appear – black felt tip works really well.
- Using single hole punchers or hole punchers that cut out different shapes (stars, hearts, etc.) to make confetti.
- Clothes pegs games – use spring-loaded clothes pegs to hang out dolls' clothes, peg out artwork to dry, etc.
- When playing with dough, give the students a garlic press to make spaghetti. This will help strengthen their hands for scissor use.

Easy cutting activities

- Snip around the edge of a piece of paper to make a pattern or snip across thin strips of paper to make a collage. This step comes before cutting across a whole page.
- Glue pieces of thin cardboard, lolly sticks or pipe cleaners or drizzle PVA glue on to sugar paper, leaving an inch or two of space down the middle. Then encourage cutting between the lines.

- Roll out dough snakes and cut into small pieces.
- Punch a hole or cluster of holes at the top and bottom of a sheet of paper and encourage students to cut from one hole to the next.
- Cut drinking straws and then thread them on to a shoelace/pipe cleaner to make jewellery.
- Make snowflakes from folded paper, using small cuts to create a design.
- Make paper chains.
- Make paper lanterns.
- Cut out pictures stuck on to card to make a jigsaw puzzle.

Cutting curves
Start with wavy thick lines before moving on to harder shapes.

- Draw a circle on a sheet of paper and lines for sunbeams. Encourage students to cut off the sunbeams by cutting the small, curved segments.
- Make spiral hanging decorations. Start with paper, then try plastic bottles to make multicoloured decorations.
- Butterfly: have your students fold paper in half, draw a shape that looks like the number '3' on one side, then cut along the line, unfold the paper and hey presto...a butterfly to decorate! Decorate with circle punch-outs from hole-punched paper or snipped magazine pages.
- Cut out shapes/pictures from greetings cards to make gift tags.

There are lots of free printable cutting sheets and craft activity ideas available on the internet.

Choosing a seasonal activity can be fun (Rangoli suncatchers and candles at Diwali, menorah decorations at Hannukah, snowflakes in winter, Easter cards made from egg-shaped card and colourful spirals for Bonfire night).

CUTLERY SKILLS

Lots of people struggle with cutlery. Mealtimes themselves can be overwhelming to students with sensory sensitivities. Add on the complex motor skills needed to use cutlery and you have a potential meltdown situation.

It is important to balance developing independence skills with the enjoyment of mealtimes and the need to intake food. It is therefore important to practise using a knife and fork away from mealtimes and through play if appropriate.

Below is a very basic guide to the skills required for effective cutting with a knife and fork.

Strategies to help

- Consider using shaped cutlery (e.g. Caring Cutlery or Nana's Manners cutlery which is shaped to guide the fingers into the correct position).
- Metal or plastic? Some students find cold metal cutlery uncomfortable in the mouth.
- Place a sticker on the index fingernail and one on the cutlery where the finger should be placed as a visual guide.
- Practise on dough. Roll a snake and cut it up.
- Start practising on soft foods such as potato croquettes, cooked carrots and bananas.
- Consider plates with a high edge or use a plate guard to stop food flying off the plate.
- Use non-slip matting under the plate to prevent it from slipping when cutting food.
- For students who prefer their food to be separated, use a sectioned portion plate.

DRESSING MILESTONES

Dressing is a complex activity. A number of skills need to be mastered in order for a child or young person to dress independently.
These include:

- Gross motor skills – for balance, coordination and strength.
- Fine motor skills – for being able to reach, grasp and release objects in order to complete tasks such as fiddly fastenings.
- Visual perception – to understand various sizes and shapes and orientation of clothing.
- Stereognosis – to be able to feel their way without relying on sight, such as finding arm holes with a jumper over their head or fastening buttons behind at the back.
- Body awareness – to be able to tell right from left and where clothing sits on the body.
- Motivation – if a student finds clothing uncomfortable or they do not have the interoception awareness of when they need to put on a coat, then dressing will need to be skilfully taught considering these differences.

12 months	Removes socks. Can put on loose-fitting hats. Helps with dressing by pushing arms through sleeves and legs through openings with clothes held for them.
2 years	Able to remove shoes and simple clothing (e.g. pyjama bottoms). Able to locate arm holes once garment over head.
2.5 years	Attempts to put on socks. Able to unbutton a large button. Able to put on easy clothing such as coat or open-front shirt but unable to fasten.
3 years	Able to put on T-shirt with a little support. Able to put on shoes, although the right and left orientation may be incorrect. Able to put on socks with a little help for the correct orientation of the heel. Able to pull zip down. Able to button large front buttons and to zip a jacket if the shank is already connected.
3.5 years	Able to unzip a jacket and separate the shank. Able to button three or four buttons. Able to find the front side/correct orientation of clothing and dress themselves with supervision.
4 years	Able to insert the shank together to zip up a jacket with practice. Able to button smaller buttons and tie shoelaces if given practice. Able to place on socks and shoes with appropriate orientation. Able to undress themselves if no tight/fiddly fastenings.
5 years	Dresses independently.

● ACTIVITIES/STRATEGIES TO SUPPORT DRESSING SKILLS

See 'Buttons made easy', 'Zip practice' and 'Shoelace tying' in the Photocopiable resources section.

- Ensure that students are sitting in a stable position (e.g. on the floor or sitting on a chair or firm bed with their feet supported). To support balance, try sitting in a corner of the room as this gives support from two walls.
- Always start with undressing as this is an easier skill.
- Play dress-up with oversized clothes and motivational costumes. Using a variety of large shirts or smocks, get students to get ready for wet play, painting or cooking.
- Teach terms 'front and back' and strategies such as the writing on the inside or sew a small thread to orientate the back. Use T-shirts with pictures on the front to support understanding of front and back.
- Use a visual support to help the order. Use photos of actual clothes to start with and move to generic pictures, line drawings and then written word.

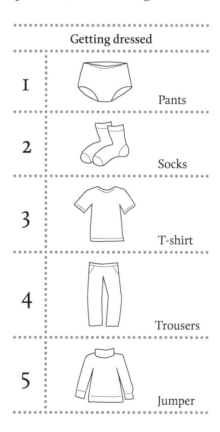

Getting dressed

1   Pants

2   Socks

3   T-shirt

4   Trousers

5   Jumper

- Matching sock game. Place a variety of socks in a pile, and the child has to find pairs and put them on.
- Play Simon Says to identify various body parts and help with body awareness.
- Complete lacing activities using lacing cards to develop fine motor skills such as grip, release and eye–hand coordination.
- Rolling/walking on various surfaces (e.g. grass, sand, rubber playground surfaces) to increase body awareness.

- Use backward chaining. Here the adult begins the task, with the child only doing the last step. Gradually, the adult does less as the child is able to do more of the task themselves. This way children always get the reward of finishing the task – for example, the adult puts the tracksuit bottoms over feet and to knees and the child then pulls up over hips.
- Choose a coat with a contrasting lining to help inside and outside.
- To help with gripping the clothes, roll the top of socks/edge of T-shirt in order to create a larger grip surface and avoid slippery/silky fabrics.
- Sport tubular socks are easier than those with a heel, and orientation will always be correct, improving the child's self-esteem.
- Socks with coloured heels and toes also make it easier to work out the correct way around.
- On the inside of shoes and trainers, mark the inside border of each piece of footwear with indelible ink. The child can then match these two marks together to ensure that the correct foot is inserted into each shoe. A small sticker on the inside edges of shoe is another idea.
- To help a child to put on a coat, drape the coat over the back of a chair with the lining facing outwards and the sleeves freely hanging. The child stands with their back to the lining and put each arm in turn into the sleeves. The child bends down to get the coat on to the shoulders and then move up and away to release the coat. Or try the 'flip it' method – place the coat on floor, children put hands/arms in sleeves and flip it over their head.

Velcro is a magnificent invention, and garments and shoes with Velcro fastenings are encouraged to preserve self-esteem.

SIMPLE STRATEGIES FOR SECONDARY SCHOOL STUDENTS

It is important to work together with your students to assist them to become aware and facilitate independent use of strategies (see the **'Self-regulation'** chapter in the **Sensory strategies** section).

- Allow time out as a time to calm, not a punishment. Use subtle strategies to allow overwhelmed students to exit class (e.g. Amazing Awareness Bands, exit cards). Make a resource by painting surfaces of a short triangular piece of wood. Paint sides red, green and yellow. If the student has the green side facing the teacher, they are feeling OK; if yellow, they are starting to feel stressed; if red, they are stressed and need to leave.
- Have a dedicated calm/wellbeing space in the school with equipment to assist calming such as beanbags, fidget/squeeze toys, mindfulness colouring books, lava lamps and options to listen to music.
- Introduce a 'buddy' system to help students navigate the school, have someone to talk to/spend time with and have as a dedicated point of contact.
- Allow students to transition to their next lesson a couple of minutes early to prevent the stressful hustle and bustle of corridors.
- Use buff-coloured paper and coloured overlays to reduce visual stress.
- Provide structured clubs during lunchtimes or a quiet place to sit with a buddy.
- Introduce yoga as a regular class/tutor group session.
- For students who doodle, provide post-it notes to doodle on rather than the student doodling on their school work.
- Provide non-obtrusive fidget toys (e.g. fidget cubes, paperclips linked together) or place rough Velcro dots on pencils and rulers for feeling.
- Allow water in sports bottles. Sucking the water is calming and assists focus.
- Chewing gum is calming and helps focus.
- Use garden swing hammocks or chair hammocks to gain calming sensory movement.
- Use calming aromatherapy sprays/spritz/pulse-point roll-ons at times of increased anxiety/stress (see 'Aromatherapy in the classroom' in the chapter **'The olfactory system'**). Bach flower remedies such as Rescue Remedy are also helpful but seek advice from establishments selling these.
- White noise and sleep story apps to assist with rest and relaxation.

- Horse riding – working with horses requires a person to be calm and focused. It also requires a lot of heavy work with feeding, grooming, mucking out and more. Lots of great sensory inputs.
- Swimming – the pressure (proprioception) of the water can be very calming and soothing to a lot of people. It is also great for fitness.
- Gardening – working in the garden involves working with differing textures, scents and other sensory inputs. It's also good physical activity with proprioceptive input for calming and regulating.
- Encourage students to use rucksacks. The weight being carried around will be calming.
- Allow a student who is hypersensitive to smell to use the staff toilets.
- Allow the use of disposable plastic gloves for messy activities such as art and food technology.

PHOTOCOPIABLE RESOURCES

*

SENSORY TREASURE CHEST

The following are examples of items that will be useful at home or in the classroom. Students will often self-select items they need to regulate their sensory systems. Many items can be bought cheaply on the high street or from reputable internet sites.

- Wobble cushion.
- Ear defenders/calming ear buds.
- Privacy board.
- Weighted items such as blankets, lap weights, weighted vests, etc.
- Large gym or 'peanut' ball.
- Trampoline/trampette.
- Swing (with a standard seat or made from a tyre).
- Vibrating cushion.
- Vibrating snake or tube.
- Vibrating creatures.
- Textured balls.
- Stress balls.
- Theraputty.
- Weighted balls.
- Tangles/fidget toys.
- Exercise bands.
- Aroma pots.
- Chewable items (commercially available).
- Koosh ball or pompom balls.
- Scented dough.
- Bubbles.
- Oil and water bottles or liquid timers.
- Glitter sticks.
- Spinning tops.
- Old CDs to spin.

Either allow the student to select an item, or have a sensory play session, where all students have time to play with the items they choose. Take note of each student's favourite items and their reaction to these items. If you see a student who is calm, or becoming calm, remember to find this item at times of stress. These items can also be used in the sanctuary area of your classroom or brought to students' desks for calming throughout the day. Put together a sensory survival kit in a drawstring bag and take it with you when away from the classroom/house.

*

SENSORY SENSITIVITY CHECKLIST

I am often asked 'Why is my student doing this...?'

The checklist below has been designed for teachers/carers. It will help you to identify why a student is displaying certain behaviour and, more importantly, which strategies you might be able to use to assist regulation. It is again important to remember that many autistic people engage in sensory behaviours to reduce anxiety or simply because they are extremely pleasurable. Be mindful of replacing behaviours because you do not see or understand the purpose. Alternatives should only be used if there is a justifiable reason to do so that will not cause further anxiety. Many outcomes can be achieved by environmental changes rather than asking the autistic person to adapt.

What you see	Possible sensory trigger	Sensory strategies
Wanting the TV or radio very loud. Seeking out or making loud noise. Making their own noise, for example humming or screaming.	Poor auditory processing/ discrimination.	Seek advice from an occupational therapist about implementing an auditory-based intervention. Provide ear defenders or a device such as an MP3 player, as the student may be making noise to mask another sound that they perceive to be threatening.
Avoiding areas that they perceive to be loud such as swimming pools or public toilets with hand dryers.	Poor auditory processing/ discrimination.	Seek advice from an occupational therapist about implementing an auditory-based intervention. Provide ear defenders or a device such as an MP3 player.
Sniffing objects, food and people.	Decreased olfactory processing.	Provide appropriate opportunities to smell things such as scented oil on a wristband, scented play dough or smell pots. Use scratch-and-sniff stickers – there are both sweet-smelling and disgusting ones on the market.
Avoiding areas with strong smells, such as toilets, farms or perfume counters.	Heightened olfactory sensitivity.	Reduce defensiveness by building up tolerance to smells – use strategies given in the box above. When out, give the students smells that they can tolerate and sniff, for example on their wristband, cuff or handkerchief.
Scratchy, fussy with clothing textures, irritated by grooming tasks or labels in clothes.	Poor tactile discrimination/ processing. Tactile sensitivity.	Seek advice from an occupational therapist about implementing the Wilbarger Protocol. Cut off tags, buy seamless clothing, turn socks inside out. Use label tape to cover itchy labels. Carry out deep-pressure massage. See the **'Proprioception – younger students'** and **'Proprioception – older students'** photocopiable sheets; carry out before the student gets dressed or does tasks such as combing their hair.

Poor or fleeting eye contact. Avoidance of 'bright' light.	Visual sensitivity.	Do not insist on eye contact, as this can be very painful and uncomfortable. Use sunglasses, caps or coloured overlays to reduce sensitivity. Interaction combined with vestibular input can improve eye contact. See **'Vestibular activities'** photocopiable sheet.
Excess fidgeting on chair/ seated on floor.	Poor proprioception and vestibular processing.	Movement breaks are essential – see **'Movement break ideas'** photocopiable sheet. Use alternative seating to give controlled movement, e.g. a wobble cushion, ball chair or wobble stool. Provide fidget toys – see **'Fidget toys'** photocopiable sheet.
Spinning.	Decreased vestibular processing. May be an element of poor visual processing.	See **'Vestibular activities'** photocopiable sheet. Provide rotatory movement, e.g. a roundabout, a spinning top or a spinning office chair. Vary the direction and carry out before periods of seated concentrated work are required.
Daredevil, reduced sense of danger, seeking rough and tumble play. Seeking firm hugs and squeezes. Poor coordination. Poor awareness of personal space.	Poor proprioception and vestibular processing.	Movement breaks are essential – see **'Movement break ideas'** photocopiable sheet. Carry out before the student is required to be seated and concentrating. Use alternative seating to give controlled movement, e.g. a wobble cushion, ball chair or wobble stool. Use weighted products (see **'Vestibular activities'**, **'Proprioception – younger students'** and **'Proprioception – older students'** photocopiable sheets). Carry out before the student is required to be seated and concentrating.
Motion sickness. Fear of heights or of falling.	Poor vestibular and visual processing.	See **'Vestibular activities'** photocopiable sheet. Use heavy work activities to calm the student's system before an event (see **'Proprioception – younger students'** and **'Proprioception – older students'** photocopiable sheets). Try pulse-point wristbands or offer ginger biscuits or stem ginger to reduce nausea.
Excessively chewing or licking anything and everything, e.g. cuffs, collars, pencils.	Decreased tactile processing especially around the mouth area. Poor proprioceptive processing. Pica – seek professional advice.	Provide commercially available items suitable for chewing, e.g. pencil toppers, chewy tubes and chewable jewellery. Give the student chewable food items such as chewy sweets and, if suitable, chewing gum. Seek advice from an occupational therapist about implementation of the Wilbarger Protocol.
Pinching or head banging.	Poor proprioceptive and tactile processing. Also consider pain and ensure the student has a way to communicate this.	See **'Proprioception – younger students'** and **'Proprioception – older students'** photocopiable sheets. Seek advice from an occupational therapist about implementation of the Wilbarger Protocol.

MESSY PLAY

∘ ∘ ∘

Young people react differently to different textures, so be aware of your students' reactions. It is essential never to force a student; allow them to lead the activity so that they can gain in confidence. If we force a student, it may lead them to resisting and becoming more sensitive to a texture. Remember that some sensations may be physically painful, so it is important that students work at their own pace.

It is also important that we show students that we enjoy messy play. This will encourage our students to enjoy it too...so no wincing and reaching immediately for hand wipes!

SUGGESTIONS FOR MESSY PLAY MATERIALS

- Dough, putty or scented dough. You can make these textured by adding sand and glitter.
- Coloured glue – sprinkle it with glitter using fingertips or a shaker.
- 'Gloop', which is home-made with cornflour and water.
- Finding objects buried in beans, rice or pasta (uncooked), or try sand or pebbles.
- Bubble play – blowing, catching, popping, etc.
- Coloured water play – use food colouring to change the colour of the water. Add bubbles, sand and/or scented oils, and make sure you have plenty of containers to pour water into, out of and through.
- Finger painting with finger paints. You can also use wet mud, shaving foam, bubbles or squirty cream.
- Papier-mâché.
- If a student is in residential accommodation, use sponges, facecloths and loofahs in the bath. Allow the student to wash themselves, dolls or bathroom tiles. This strategy can also be used at home.
- Feely bags or treasure baskets – place lots of different shapes and textures in a bag and ask students to find a specific item. No peeking!
- Encourage messy play in the bath where something can immediately be washed off if it bothers students. Use body crayons, shaving foam or liquid soap.
- Pasta play – put some cooked pasta on a table or into an empty water tray for students to explore.
- Add toys to the pasta to add to their enjoyment and learning opportunities. You might use various shapes and sizes of containers, mega blocks or animals.
- Tactile path – place food with different textures into large trays. Examples are wet pasta or spaghetti, dry pasta, rice and jelly. Have students walk barefoot, or on hands and knees, through the trays.
- Mousse play – make up some mousse in a bowl, according to the instructions on the packet. Once the mousse has set, tip it on to a table or into a messy tray. Place toys

into the mousse, such as tea sets, mega blocks or plastic animals. Allow students to explore the mousse using these items, plus their senses of touch, smell and taste.

♦ Cooked pasta play – make large quantities of cooked spaghetti or other types of pasta, adding food colouring to the cooking water if you wish. Add small creatures, puzzle pieces, etc. to the cooked pasta. Try making blue spaghetti, putting it in a paddling pool and adding sea creatures. Offer some kitchen tools and saucepans for pretend play and developing hand control – try strainers, tongs, spoons, tweezers and pasta tongs. Alternatively, add spaghetti to a water tray and watch what happens as the pasta dissolves in water. See the **'Food play activities'** photocopiable sheet for more ideas.

*

FOOD PLAY ACTIVITIES

Food play sessions can help to reduce the fear of food. Let students work at their own pace and touch, sniff and explore the food as much as they want to. Never force a student to eat the food during these sessions. If a student does try to eat some of the food, this is seen as a bonus.

IDEAS FOR FOOD PLAY

Custard, yoghurt or squirty cream play

Pour tins of custard (yoghurt and cream are good alternatives) into a water tray or smaller messy play trays. Allow students to make a mess exploring the texture, taste and smell of the custard. Add toys for them to play with. Use your fingers to draw shapes, handprints and footprints.

Dry pasta or rice play

Put some pasta or rice on to a table or into a tray for students to explore. Add toys to the pasta to add to their enjoyment and learning opportunities, such as various shapes and sizes of containers, mega blocks or animals. Use this as a lucky dip or as a way of finding pieces to complete a jigsaw puzzle. Once students are happy to explore the dry food, wet their hands so pieces stick to them.

Cornflour 'gloop'

Make gloop by mixing cornflour and water together. This creates an amazing substance unlike any other! Put the gloop in large trays or onto a table and encourage students to play with it. They will enjoy just touching it, picking it up, moving it around and letting it drizzle through their fingers. Gloop goes hard when you roll it into a ball and turns back to liquid once you keep it still.

Enjoy making patterns in the gloop and just watching them disappear. Add some food colouring for a different experience. Add sand for texture or scented oils. This is also great for practising letter formation.

Mousse play

Make up the mousse in a bowl, according to the instructions on the packet. Once the mousse has set, tip it on to a table or into a messy tray. Place toys in the mousse such as tea sets, mega blocks or plastic animals. Allow students to explore the mousse using these items and their senses of touch, smell and taste. You could also use it as a lucky dip or do handprints or footprints on large pieces of paper.

Tactile path

Place food with different textures in large trays, such as wet pasta or spaghetti, dry pasta, rice and jelly. Have students walk barefoot or on their hands and knees through the trays.

Cooked pasta play

Make large quantities of cooked spaghetti or other types of pasta, adding colouring to the cooking water if you wish. Add small creatures to the cooked pasta – try making blue spaghetti, putting it in a paddling pool and adding sea creatures.

Offer some kitchen tools and saucepans for pretend play. Try using strainers, tongs, spoons, tweezers and pasta tongs. Dip the cooked pasta in paint and trail it across a page. Or walk in trays of cooked pasta.

Vegetable printing

Dip cut potatoes, carrots or broccoli into paint and make patterns.

Cream or shaving foam

Choose allergen-free shaving foams and check that students are not dairy intolerant before using products such as instant or whipped cream. Place the substance on tables or upright surfaces such as mirrors, walls or windows. Draw shapes with fingers or use the cream to decorate biscuits.

Alternatively, place foam in deeper trays and create a treasure hunt for students by hiding buttons, pebbles, coins, big beads, small figures and so on in the tray. Add texture by using glitter, pasta, lentils, sand or beads. Add colours (paint or food colouring) to explore colour mixing and colour changing.

Marshmallow fun

Make animals and shapes out of marshmallows by stacking onto dried pasta or skewers.

Fruit and vegetable faces

Using a variety of fruits and vegetables (the more interesting shapes the better), carve, cut, slice and dice your way to making interesting faces, animals and other everyday items. Dip into paint to make pictures with the shapes. Dip into melted chocolate to add a different flavour.

Mash up

Mash soft fruit and make paths for toy cars to drive through.

MOVEMENT BREAK IDEAS

We all have different levels of alertness, which affect our ability to concentrate, listen to instructions and focus to complete our work. Following periods of seated work, students need a movement break to regulate and re-focus.

Choose an activity from the list below. Each activity should last for a minimum of one to two minutes to be effective.

- ◆ Run or jog around the playground or use outdoor gyms.
- ◆ Get students to carry heavy notebooks to the office or from class to class. Set up a fake reason for them to take books as far as possible around the school, then swap with another teacher to bring books back.
- ◆ Jump up and down on a trampoline or do star/jack jumps.
- ◆ Bounce (seated) on a large ball. Bounce in a circle while seated, lift alternate legs, play throw, etc.
- ◆ Do Theraband exercises. See if students can pull their hands away from each other, thereby placing resistance on the band. Then slowly release the tension on the band. Try for ten pulls. Then slowly release.
- ◆ Get students to hold therapy balls with their arms and legs while lying on their backs. Tell them to hold on to the ball as hard as they can while you try to take it away.
- ◆ Try cross crawling. March on the spot, touching elbow or hand to opposite leg as high as possible. Start with eyes open and then try with eyes closed. March on the spot and then try to turn in a circle.
- ◆ Do weight-bearing exercises for the arms, such as the wheelbarrow walk, crab walk or bear walk. Alternatively, use a ball as shown below: move forward and backwards over the ball using the arms. Play a game in this position.
- ◆ Move a ball slowly from side to side, forwards and backwards (see below).

- ◆ Logroll: lying on the floor, roll across a mat while trying to keep the body in a straight line. Advance by extending arms above head or extending the distance of the roll.

＊

◆ Wall pushes: do 20 push-ups against the wall. Make sure elbows are bending and straightening rather than the whole body.

◆ Use weights: hold a small weight in each hand (you could use filled tins, water bottles, etc.). Keep arms extended above the head and/or held parallel for as long as possible.

◆ Steamroller: with students lying down, roll a large ball up and down their body. Keep pressure firm.

*

SCOOTER BOARD ACTIVITIES

o 100 o

- ◆ Push a scooter board to, or from, a designated location (students can sit, or lie on their stomachs and propel themselves with their arms).
- ◆ Students can try pulling themselves up a ramp while seated or lying on their stomachs on a scooter board.
- ◆ Students can also try propelling a scooter board across a carpeted floor, alternating arms or using both arms together.
- ◆ Have one student use a rope or plastic hoop to pull another student who is sitting or lying (on their stomach) on a scooter board and holding onto the other end of the rope or hoop.
- ◆ Also see 'Scooter Board Activities' later in this section.

DAILY SENSORY SESSIONS

Sensory input is a natural, calming sensation for the brain. We all need sensory input to stay calm and focused – ideally, sensory sessions should run first thing each morning and after lunch breaks. **Sessions should take approximately 10–15 minutes**. Set equipment up in sections: each student needs to complete one activity from each section in strict order.

You could try organising activities into three main sections: alerting, organising and calming. It's best to finish sensory sessions with calming activities. The ideas below are based on work by the occupational therapist Jane Norwood, as found in her book *Sensory Circuits* (2009).

ALERTING

Jogging
Jog on the spot or inside a hoop. Advance by changing speed up and down, or jogging around a course of cones.

Star jumps
Start by doing arms and legs separately if coordination is poor. Advance by turning in circles, going side to side and/or counting while jumping.

Jack jumps
Jump from a crouched position with arms and legs out to the side, then return to the crouched position. Advance by combining with jogging.

Ball bounce
Bounce while seated on an exercise ball. Advance by bouncing for longer without stopping, bouncing while turning around on the ball, or throwing and catching items (such as a beanbag or a smaller ball) while bouncing.

Arm spinning
Stand with arms stretched out to the sides. Spin in a circle ten times one way and then reverse.

Trampoline
Bounce on the spot, around in circles, do star jumps.

*

ORGANISING

Logroll

Lie on the floor and roll across a mat while trying to keep the body in a straight line. Advance by extending arms above the head or extending the distance of the roll.

Cross crawling

March on the spot, touching elbow or hand to opposite leg as high as possible. Start with eyes open and then try with eyes closed. March on the spot and then try to turn in a circle.

Juggling

Start with throwing and catching silk scarves as they move very slowly. Move on to beanbags and then juggling balls.

Commando crawling

Lie on the stomach and crawl across the ground. Try having a race or crawling under blankets.

Oral motor

Blow whistles, blow feathers off your hand, play football by blowing a cotton ball or ping pong ball across a table (you score if you blow it off the other end).

Rolling over a ball

Lie on the stomach over a peanut ball and walk hands back and forth.

Lazy eight

Use ribbons or scarves, or use chalk on a large vertical surface to draw out figures of eight. Make sure that students cross their midline by keeping their hips still and facing frontwards.

Balance obstacle course

Walk along a balance beam, bench, stepping stones or a line taped on the floor. Advance by walking backwards, stepping over objects along the way, bending down to pick up beanbags to throw at targets.

＊

CALMING

Steamroller
Students lie on their tummies while an adult rolls a large exercise ball slowly up and down them.

Wall pushes
Do 20 push-ups against a wall. Make sure that students' elbows are bending and straightening rather than their whole body. You can also try this with two students pushing against each other's hands or feet.

Pushing or pulling weighted items
Try using a full wheelbarrow, filled bags, etc. Make this into a game by asking students to fetch certain items to fill the bag or barrow.

Pilates plank
Students lie on their stomachs on the floor, come up on to their forearms and on to their toes (stomach, thighs and chest off floor).

Calming yoga
See the **'Relaxation yoga'** photocopiable sheet.

Massage
There are many forms of massage that can be calming and help students to re-focus. The Massage in Schools programme allows students to massage each other, which promotes self-esteem. See **https://misa.org.uk** for more details.

Press-ups

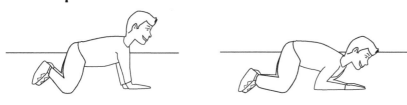

Using weights
Hold a small weight in each hand (you could use filled tins or water bottles). Hold arms extended above the head or parallel for as long as possible.

PROPRIOCEPTION – YOUNGER STUDENTS

Proprioceptive input (sensations from joints, muscles and connective tissues that lead to body awareness) can be obtained by lifting, pushing and pulling heavy objects, including one's own weight. Students can also stimulate the proprioceptive sense by engaging in activities that push joints together (such as pushing something heavy), or that pull joints apart (such as hanging from monkey bars).

Carry out two activities from the ideas in this worksheet and **'Proprioception – older students'** at the beginning of each school day, after playtime and throughout the day if necessary to calm and focus students.

Play in a ball pool

Lie under blankets and cushions
Always make sure that students can move freely and that their heads are not covered at any time.

Monkey bars or climbing frames

Steamroller
With students lying down, roll a large ball up and down their bodies. Keep pressure firm.

Weights
Hold a small weight in each hand (e.g. filled tins or water bottles). Hold arms extended above the head or parallel for as long as possible. Lift bottles filled with water up and down to shoulders, 15 times.

Trampoline

Arm circles
Ten each way – keep arms straight!

Gym ball

Bounce up and down, bounce around an obstacle course, lie over the ball and play a game.

Lycra body sox

While in the body sox, do relay races, jack jumps, crawling, etc.

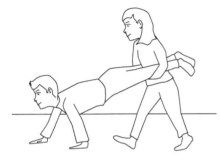

Wheelbarrow walks

Crawling

Crawl under blankets, through tunnels and under bean-bags. Try crawling on stomachs, on all fours or like a crab.

Theraband activities

Do each exercise ten times.

Blowing bubbles

Manipulating putty

Hide objects in putty or enjoy pulling and twisting it around.

PROPRIOCEPTION – OLDER STUDENTS

Proprioceptive input (sensations from joints, muscles and connective tissues that lead to body awareness) can be obtained by lifting, pushing and pulling heavy objects, including one's own weight. Students can also stimulate the proprioceptive sense by engaging in activities that push joints together (such as pushing something heavy) or pull joints apart (such as hanging from monkey bars).

Carry out two activities from those below at the beginning of each school day and after playtime if necessary, to calm and focus students. Also see the **'Core stability'** photocopiable sheet below.

Heavy lifting
Without straining, students can lift free weights. Start with 0.5 kg. Lift above the head ten times, so the bicep curls ten times.

Arm circles
Ten each way – keep arms straight!

Push-ups and stabilisation
Do ten push-ups. Carry out in four-point kneeling to aid stability if it is too difficult or over a ball or bolster. Try doing ten opposite leg/arm lifts.

Lycra body sox
While in the body sox, do relay races, jack jumps, crawling, etc.

Push a gym ball up and down the wall
Carry out with each arm and then with the back. Don't let the ball drop! Move the ball up and down the wall five times.

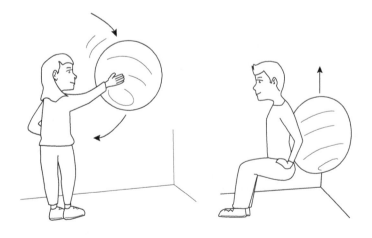

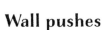

Wall pushes
Do ten pushes. Keep feet flat!

Chair push-ups
Do ten push-ups while seated on a chair.

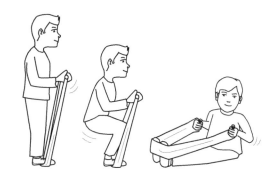

Theraband activities
Try ten of each exercise.

Hit a punch bag

OTHER SUGGESTED ACTIVITIES

- ◆ Riding a bike.
- ◆ Hanging from monkey bars.
- ◆ Lying under heavy or weighted blankets.
- ◆ Bouncing on a gym ball.
- ◆ Having a tug o'war.
- ◆ Wrapping up tightly in a blanket, duvet or sleeping bag.
- ◆ Outdoor/indoor gyms.

*

VESTIBULAR ACTIVITIES

Activities that are vestibular in nature increase input to the vestibular system and help to increase students' arousal levels.

The general rule is that linear movement (side to side, up and down) is calming, and rotary movement (round and round) is alerting. It's a good idea for students to have movement breaks before they settle to academic tasks.

Allow students to stand as much as possible when working on activities that require periods of concentration. This requires greater movement, which in turn will activate brain stem activity.

IDEAS FOR VESTIBULAR ACTIVITIES

- Playground swing: if students propel these themselves, this is 'heavy' work and therefore calming.
- See-saws.
- Slides, whether sitting, lying down or going head first.
- Zip wires.
- Trampolines: bouncing is good, and you can add an alerting component by asking students to bounce around in circles.
- Rocking chairs can be useful in the corner of a classroom for calming.
- Hanging upside down over balls or from playground equipment.
- Hammock swings.
- Dancing to music.
- Trampolining.
- Somersaulting and general gymnastic movements.
- Spin on the stomach or upright on a computer chair.
- Balancing, seated, on gym balls and reaching for objects. Slowly increase the reaching distance. Encourage students to reach in the air, to either side and from the ground to stimulate their vestibular systems.

Scooter board activities

- Using a scooter board, have students become animals while lying forward on the board. Then ask students to be animals lying on their backs, using scooter boards to get around.
- Lie on scooter boards and negotiate a coned path. Collect beanbags on the way.
- Ask students to lie or sit on the board and hold on to a rope or plastic hoop. Pull them along yourself or have other students pull them.

*

Inner tube activities

- ◆ Use an old tyre inner tube (tractor tyre inner tubes are perfect) and have students sit on the tube and bounce. While they are sitting, throw beanbags into a target.
- ◆ Suggest that students jump in and out of the tube or practise their balancing by walking around the edge of the tube.

Logrolls

- ◆ Lying on the floor, roll across a mat while trying to keep the body in a straight line. Advance by extending arms above the head or extending the distance of the roll.
- ◆ Trampolines: have a small indoor trampoline on which students can jump, twist and catch or throw balls. Get students to sit on the trampoline and bounce on it. Bounce from standing to sitting and vice versa; you can also try jogging on the spot and turning around.

CALMING ACTIVITIES

*

- Bounce around a coned course on a space hopper or gym ball – 10–15 trips should take all the frustration out of students and allow them to focus on the task in hand.
- Push a large therapy ball across or around a room (you can buy weighted therapy balls). An adult or another pupil can add resistance by pushing lightly in the opposite direction.
- Play catch with a heavy ball or medicine ball. Bounce and roll the ball.
- Push a wheeled stool while someone is sitting on it. If necessary, the person on the stool can help by 'walking' with their feet.
- Use a Theraband or tubing attached to a door and pull it, then let it snap.
- Two children can play tug o' war together using a skipping rope.
- Play jumping games, such as hopscotch and skipping.
- Rub out chalk or pen from boards in the classroom.
- Ask students to help rearrange desks or chairs in the classroom. Alternatively, stack chairs.
- Carry books with both hands, hugging books to the chest.
- Use squeeze toys that can be squeezed quietly on students' laps under their desk, so that the class isn't disturbed.
- Do chair push-ups.
- Jump on a trampoline.
- Do press-ups against a wall. Make sure that students' feet are flat on the ground and movement is coming from bending elbows.
- Carry heavy items, such as a washing basket, shopping bags or buckets of water.
- Rake grass or leaves, push a wheelbarrow, dig soil or wash the car. Try animal walks.
- **Frog jump:** squat on the floor, placing hands on floor in front. Move both hands forward, then bring feet up to hands in jumping motion (remain in squatting position).
- **Bear walk:** with hands and feet on floor, move right arm and leg forward simultaneously, then move left arm and leg. If this is too difficult, try it on hands and knees.
- **Caterpillars:** squat on floor with hands in front. Keeping feet stable, walk hands forward as far as you can so that you are stretched out. Then keep hands stable and walk feet up to hands and back to squatting position.
- **Kangaroo jump:** squat on floor, hands at sides, raise up and jump forward, sinking back into squatting position as you land.
- **Crab walk:** lean back and put hands on floor (facing up with buttocks off floor); walk backwards using hands and feet alternately.
- **Duck walk:** squat on floor with hands at sides. Remain in position while walking (waddling) forward.
- **Elephant walk:** bend over with arms dangling toward floor. Clasp hands together to form trunk. Maintain position while walking and swinging trunk from side to side.

*

FIDGET TOYS

Many students who are easily distracted seek out sensation and need to fidget to maintain focus and attention.

Providing a 'fidget toy' can provide this input in a non-distracting way. By using a fidget toy, students can filter out the extra sensory information.

The majority of autistic students or those with attention deficit hyperactivity disorder (ADHD) and sensory processing differences are prone to be both distracted and distractible. A fidget toy for the classroom needs to be quiet, inexpensive and safe.

Students should be allowed to choose their own fidget toy as only they know exactly what will satisfy that need to fidget.

IDEAS FOR FIDGET TOYS

- Fidget cube.
- Spinners such as starfish.
- Blu Tack.
- Hand exercisers.
- Acupressure rings.
- Pencil top fidgets.
- Pocket fidgets such as the Ultimate Fidget.
- Retractable key fobs.
- Pieces of string or ribbon.
- Paperclips slotted together.
- Bubble wrap (but not in a quiet classroom!).
- Stress balls.
- Bumpy shells.
- Smooth stones.

- Beads.
- A rubber band ball.
- Bendable dolls.
- Stretchy people or animal figures.
- Sand timers.
- Bendy straws.
- Beanbags.
- A rubber band around a pencil.
- Tangle toys.
- Rough Velcro dots placed on underside of desks or on rulers.
- Commercially available fidget pencil cases.
- Rubber charity bracelets.
- Putty.

Consider students' safety when choosing a fidget toy as some toys could be a choking hazard. Allergies also need to be considered as some squeeze ball contents may contain nut oils, etc.

*

CORE STABILITY

Ideally this routine should be carried out at least three times a week. Remember to breathe! Have students count out loud to assist with breath control.

IDEAS FOR CORE STABILITY

Bridging

Lift and hold for five seconds. Carry out ten times. Make sure knees are tight together – hold a ball/beanbag between the knees to encourage this. Increase difficulty by passing a beanbag around the hips while they are raised or place feet on a wobble cushion. Once mastered, move onto the moves below.

Four-point kneeling
Hold for five seconds. Swap sides. Carry out ten times on each side. Increase difficulty by placing knee or hand on wobble cushion.

Plank
Work up to holding for 60 seconds.
    Start with lifting arms, then arms and head and then all together. This is a good calming activity, too.

Superman stretch
Start by lifting just arms, hold for five seconds and repeat ten times. Once mastered, lift head and finally lift legs.

Curl up
Try and hold for ten seconds without rolling to the side, stretch out and curl up again. Repeat ten times. Increase difficulty by letting go of legs and placing arms crossed over chest.

Other activities along with yoga, gym ball activities and balance activities that will target core stability are:

Wall sit – hold for 30 seconds

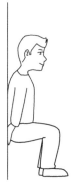

High kneeling

One leg high kneeling

Playing lying on tummy

Mountain climbers

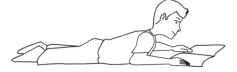

Theraband exercises

Try to pull hands away from each other, thereby placing resistance on the band and then slowly release the tension on the band. Try for ten pulls.

Animal walks
(See **'Calming activities'**.)

Crab walking
Walk ten paces across the room, backwards, forwards and sideways. Remember to keep hips in the air. Increase difficulty by carrying a beanbag on the stomach.

*

PROGRESSIVE MUSCLE RELAXATION

Progressive relaxation techniques are an effective way to manage stress with students of all ages and can be carried out at home and school. For students who have difficulties falling asleep, these exercises may aid relaxation at bedtime.

This is a useful and easy relaxation technique. It was developed by American physician Edmund Jacobson in the early 1920s and, along with aiding relaxation, it helps students be aware of their bodies and tension they hold within particular muscle groups. Keep your voice quiet and your speech slow as you guide students through the routine.

THE ROUTINE

Find a quiet and comfortable place to lie down. Start by taking some deep breaths: in through the nose and a big sigh to let it out.

Eyes closed only if students are comfortable with this.

1. Concentrate on the muscles in your face. Clench your teeth tightly together and then relax. Next screw up your eyes and face tightly, then relax.
2. Bring your shoulders tightly up towards your ears, now relax them down.
3. Next, feel your tummy. Place one hand right above your belly button. Breathe in deeply and let out the breath slowly. Notice how your tummy rises and falls. (Repeat at least ten times.) Squeeze your tummy in, hold, then let it go.
4. Now move to your arms and hands. Make a fist and squeeze tightly. Relax and let arms and hands relax.
5. Move down to your toes. Scrunch up your toes and squeeze your legs together, hold, then release.
6. Now let your whole body go limp. Notice how this feels and breathe slowly. After a short time, slowly encourage students to open their eyes. It may be best to count down to this to give some warning.

*

RELAXATION YOGA

As we know, autistic children and young people often experience the world in a heightened and overwhelming manner. This can result in their bodies becoming stuck in fight, flight or freeze modes. This results in an increased heart rate and shallower breathing, which increases anxiety levels.

Carrying out a simple yoga routine can have these benefits:

◆ improved flexibility, strength, balance, coordination, and body awareness
◆ improved core and trunk stability including posture
◆ balancing poses require concentration, which is calming
◆ increased self-confidence
◆ stretching poses relieve mental and physical tension
◆ enhances a calm and alert state in readiness to learn
◆ aids self-regulation
◆ can facilitate a restful night's sleep if carried out at bedtime.

Never force any of these positions – just remind everyone to breathe quietly and calmly. Encourage long deep breaths as lengthening the breath moves us from a fight-or-flight state to a rest-and-calm state.

YOGA ROUTINES

Diamond
Take five deep breaths in through the nose and out through the mouth.

Butterfly pose
Take five deep breaths in through the nose and out through the mouth.

Child pose
Be quiet and still.

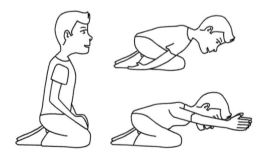

Cat/dog pose
Repeat sequence five times.

Downward dog
Hold for five seconds.

Tree
Breathe in and out and raise your hands up to the sky. Lift right leg to your knee. Place your right foot back on the mat and do the same on the other side.

Lie down
Close your eyes, let your body 'flop' and breathe deeply.

*

SELF JOINT COMPRESSIONS

Many individuals with sensory processing differences find deep pressure calming. Teaching them to use the techniques below may help them when they feel overwhelmed.

IDEAS FOR COMPRESSIONS

Arms 1
Press your hands together firmly ten times.

Arms 2
Stand with feet flat on the floor. Push the wall – bend and straighten your elbows.

Legs 1
Sit down with your legs at a 90-degree angle. Place your palms on the tops of your knees and press down on your knees (toward the floor) ten times.

Legs 2
Stand with one foot on the wall. Lean your weight forward and push your foot against the wall ten times. Swap legs and repeat.

Shoulders
Sit down, cross arms and place on opposite shoulders. Pull down firmly on shoulders. Hold for a couple of seconds and then repeat ten times.

Head
Very easy. Just stand or sit up straight, cup both your hands over your head and push downward ten times. Cup front and back of head and squeeze ten times.

*

INFINITY WALK

The infinity walk and method was conceived in the mid-1980s by clinical psychotherapist, Deborah Sunbeck (2002). It is a simple movement pattern that can be described as walking in a figure of eight while looking off at a 90-degree angle towards a target from the figure-of-eight path.

The infinity walk aids 'learning readiness', targeting attention and focus as well as balance, motor coordination and visual skills. It is a challenge that incorporates physical and cognitive skills, thus improving the body's overall coordination.

This exercise also improves visual skills as well as full body awareness. It is a great exercise for all ages!

A beginner student aims to walk smoothly in a figure-of-eight pattern around two points while looking at an object or person across the room placed at 90 degrees to the centre of the 8.

As they become able to do that consistently, other physical and mental activities can be added to the coordinated walking. Students can read from a chart held up by an adult (e.g. numbers, shapes, colours). Once they can maintain a smooth figure-of-eight walk while reading from the chart, more advanced activities can be added such as copying gestures and doing spellings/mental arithmetic as they walk.

HOW TO DO IT

- Place two small chairs/objects three feet apart.
- Beginning in the middle of the two objects, the student starts walking around the chairs in a figure-of-eight pattern outside and then inside the chairs.
- As the student walks the pattern, they should never lose sight of the target being held by an adult.
- Once the pattern is well established, the student can read attached charts while walking.

SCOOTER BOARD ACTIVITIES

Scooter board activities help:

- upper extremity strengthening
- core strengthening
- sensory motor – proprioception and vestibular
- motor planning
- bilateral coordination
- visual perceptual skills.

Scooter munch

Place some balls/beanbags in the middle of the room. Split the class into teams. When you say 'go', each team pushes a rider on a scooter towards the middle. They try to capture as many balls as possible, either with a laundry basket or with their hands. Each team then pulls the rider back either by holding their feet or pulling on rope. Keep going until most of the balls have been captured – the team with the most balls wins! A great team game!

Bowling

Set up bowling pins/stacking cups at one end of the room, and have students ride the scooter board down to knock them over or roll a ball at the pins.

Fishing

Scatter magnetic fish around the floor and have students go and find them with a magnet on a string.

Pull around with a rope or a hula hoop

Races

Do a puzzle

Have the puzzle pieces at one end of the room, and the puzzle board at the other end.

Obstacle courses of increasing complexity

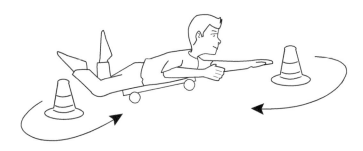

Follow a path of tape placed on the floor

Cross-country skiing

Holding sink plungers, sit cross-legged or lie on tummy on the scooter boards. Have students scoot to one side of the room, pick up an object and bring it back, race peers or follow taped path all while 'skiing' with the plungers.

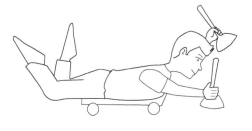

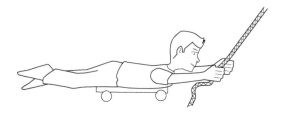

Rope pull

Have students pull themselves along a rope on tummy or above head if lying on back.

THERAPY GYM BALL ACTIVITIES

These activities will target core/postural stability, strength, coordination and proprioception.

- ◆ Balancing seated on ball and reaching for objects. Transfer objects from one box to another using tongs and progressing to tweezers. Find pegs hidden in putty, throw and catch ball/beanbag, manipulate coins from palm of hand into pot.

- ◆ Sit on ball, lift alternate feet and hold for ten seconds. Have the students kick a ball at a target or bounce around in a circle in both directions.

- ◆ Sit on ball and hold leg out straight for ten seconds, alternate legs. Hold a small hoop over ankle once able to hold without difficulty. Kick a small ball at a target.

- ◆ Lie over ball, lift alternate leg and arm, and hold for ten seconds on each side. Repeat three times.

- ◆ Move forward and backwards using only arms. Carry out pegging type activity in this position, rubber band board or bowling a small ball at a target or skittles.

- Push-ups over ball.

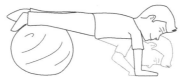

- Feet on ball, move ball from side to side without feet leaving the ball.

- Lift foot off ball and hold for ten seconds. Keep ball still with other leg. Carry out both sides.

- Bridging. Lift hips but keep ball still. Once able to lift hips without difficulty, lift hips and one leg. Hold leg in air for ten seconds, repeat on other side. Try to keep a beanbag on your tummy!

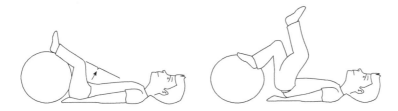

- Ball lifting. Carry out slowly. If playing with peers, pass on down the line and back. Use legs or arms.

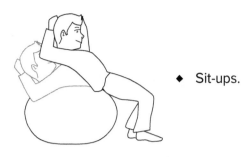

◆ Sit-ups.

◆ Wall ball – move it up and down the wall. Don't let it drop.

FINE MOTOR SKILLS ACTIVITIES

Good fine motor skills are essential for many activities including handwriting, dressing, typing and manipulation tasks. The activities below need to be regularly incorporated into students' days to increase fine motor dexterity.

◆ Clothes pegs opened with the thumb and index finger help to strengthen pincer grip.

◆ Pick small items (e.g. buttons, beads) out of play dough with the thumb and index finger. Race against peers!

◆ Play dough – roll into snakes and cut with knife and fork or plastic scissors. Let students play with cookie cutters/play dough cutters, rolling pins, etc. Squeeze, flatten and roll. Use a garlic press to squeeze dough through.

◆ Tape paper to a flat wall surface for drawing or writing – assists shoulder stability.

◆ Cut drinking straws and then lace on string. String macaroni or buttons on to dry spaghetti, pipe cleaner or thread.

◆ Have students screw/unscrew nuts and bolts. Use construction kits.

◆ Tool use, such as hammering or using a screwdriver.

◆ Rice bucket filled with parquetry shapes, plastic animals, puzzle pieces, shapes that the children can identify with eyes closed.

◆ Screw lids on and off jars. You can add interest to this activity by hiding small objects or stickers inside the jar for students to discover.

◆ Tweezer games. Move objects from one container to another. There are lots of commercially available games using tweezers.

◆ Posting games like pennies in a piggy bank. Hold pennies in hand and only use index finger and thumb to manipulate into slot without dropping the coins held in the hand.

◆ Tear strips of paper, crumple up using tips of fingers and paste on paper to make a collage.

◆ Loop rubber band around pencil several times. Using only one hand for both holding and manipulating, move rubber band to other end of pencil.

◆ Place rubber band around fingers and stretch fingers in and out.

◆ Play travel-sized games, especially Connect 4. For added challenge, you must play with only the amount of chips you can hold from the start.

◆ Use chopsticks to eat popcorn, raisins, peas, etc.

◆ Origami activities.

◆ Have the child mix two colours of dough/clay together to get a new colour. It takes quite a bit of kneading to blend them well.

◆ Make coil pots with clay.

◆ Use hole punch to punch a design in coloured paper. Make into a paper lantern.

◆ Using the side of a crayon, rub over a leaf, coin or brass rubbing to make a design on paper.

◆ Use a bulb syringe to blow cotton balls across a table.

*

BILATERAL COORDINATION
(USING TWO HANDS)

- Tear strips of paper and paste on to paper to make a collage.
- Squeeze, push and pull on clay, putty, play dough or modelling foam.
- Pull apart construction toys (DUPLO®, LEGO®) with both hands.
- Roll play dough, putty or clay with rolling pins.
- Play percussion toys: cymbals, drums (both hands together), etc.
- Penny flipping: line up a row of pennies, start flipping coins using both hands from outside coin to the centre.
- Lacing activities: lacing cards, lace art boards, etc.
- Games to help promote this skill include: Bop It, Mr Potato Head (make sure students stabilise the head with one hand while placing body parts with the other hand), Rubik's cube, Etch-A-Sketch, rhythm sticks, LEGO®.
- Ball and balloon games: have students use both hands to pass the ball or balloon overhead, between legs, roll at a target.
- Ball play: throw and catch with both hands together.
- Spring-loaded clothes pegs.
- Bounce a large ball with two hands; throw or push a ball with two hands.
- Cut out all types of things with scissors: cut straws and then string up pieces for jewellery, cut play dough or putty, cut up greeting cards and make a collage.
- Spread butter, or any spread, on crackers, ice biscuits or cookies; be sure to hold the cracker or biscuit still.
- Trace around stencils: the helper hand holds the stencil down firmly while the other draws around the stencils.
- Marching to music and clapping hands at the same time.
- Cross crawls – touch your right hand to your left knee and then the left hand to your right knee. Repeat touching the opposite feet.
- Traditional jumping jacks.
- Cross-country jumping jacks: place right arm and right leg forward, jump and switch left arm and left leg forward. Try opposite sides place right arm and left leg forward, jump and switch left arm and right leg forward.
- March in place sitting down while drawing circles in the air with both hands.
- Pulling on a rope is a good way to get the hands working rhythmically together.

*

MULTISENSORY APPROACH
TO HANDWRITING

VISUAL

- Write or scribble on different kinds of paper (e.g. regular, sugar, greaseproof, foil, brown paper), whiteboards, chalkboards, etc.
- Use different writing implements such as paintbrush, chalk, wax crayons, wide markers, colour-changing pens, metallic pens, light-up pens and vibrating pens.
- Use special colouring books in which the colour appears when students paint with water or the picture appears when you scratch through the black layer.

TACTILE

- Finger painting in paint, shaving foam, whipped cream, talcum powder and cornflour gloop.
- Draw on surfaces with different textures such as sandpaper and textured wallpaper.
- Trace over letters made from sandpaper, pipe cleaners, drizzled and dried PVA glue, dough.
- Add sand to finger paints to increase feedback.

OLFACTORY

- Drawing with scented markers, pens, pencils and crayons.
- Add food flavourings such as vanilla and peppermint to finger paints or a few drops of bubble bath or scented oils to home-made finger paints.
- Draw in scented lotions spread out on a table/tray.

AUDITORY

- Use a musical toothbrush to paint.
- Attach bells to a paintbrush or use a pencil topper with bells attached.
- Draw and paint to music following the rhythm.

GUSTATORY

- Draw frosting on a cake to decorate it. Decorate biscuits with icing tubes.
- Finger painting in whipped cream, yoghurt, Angel Delight, flat layers of jelly.
- Draw on crackers and toast with tubes of cheese spread.
- Use sweet laces to form letters.

PROPRIOCEPTION

- Use a weighted pen or paint with a weighted paintbrush. Add weight by wrapping lots of elastic bands around or taping coins to the stem.
- Vibrating pens.
- Write while wearing wrist weights.
- Write shapes, letters and words in the air with ribbon sticks, scarves and sparklers.

VESTIBULAR

- Walk, run, skip, jump, ride a scooter board around shapes and letters marked out on the floor.
- Make your body into a shape. Can be done alone or as a team game.

*

HANDWRITING WARM-UP

o 129 o

Doing some fun warm-up activities prior to handwriting practice or any activity requiring fine motor skills can help students to prepare mentally and physically. They will increase alertness levels and warm up the muscles. This routine should take no longer than five minutes.

START IN STANDING POSITION

Arm circles
Arms kept straight and stretched out to the side.

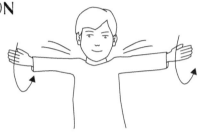

Lazy eights
Arm straight out in front and hand held in a thumbs-up position. Trace large 'lazy eights' in the air. Keep hips still so that the drawing hand crosses the middle of the body. Perform five, then change arms.

Track your hand with your eyes but keep your head still.

Sitting on chair
Feet well supported on floor or box.

Chair push-ups
Put your hands on either side of the chairs that you are sitting on and push, until your bottom rises off the chair. Once strong enough, try to hold body in the air for a few seconds.

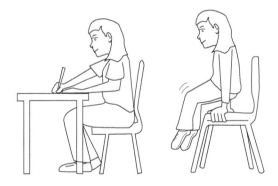

Hand sparkles
Clench both hands to make a fist, then release and stretch fingers out. Repeat five times.

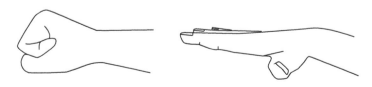

Twisting

Place forearms on desk, arms in front of you with palms facing upwards. Keep your fingers together and your thumbs open. Turn both hands over at the wrist so that palms touch the desk. Repeat back and forth ten times.

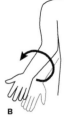

A   B

Finger opposition

Oppose thumb to each finger from index to little finger and back. Repeat three times.

Caterpillar

Writing hand only – walk your fingers up and down the pencil (your index finger will look like a caterpillar climbing the pencil).

PUTTY IDEAS FOR HAND STRENGTHENING

Putty can be used to improve grip strength, dexterity and hand strength. Improving these skills will affect all fine motor activities such as handwriting, fiddly fastenings and grasping cutlery.

If there are sensitivities to the texture of the putty, then it can be put in a plastic ziplock bag or covered with clingfilm.

ACTIVITY IDEAS

- Make your name out of putty. Take small pieces of putty, roll into a snake and make the letters of name, age, pet's name, etc.
- Hide and seek: hide small objects (beads, marbles, coins) inside the putty and then try pulling and pinching them out. Increase challenge by adding a timer and trying to beat best time to retrieve objects.
- Make a doughnut: roll the putty into a ball using both hands. Roll the ball into a snake. Squish ends together to form a doughnut. Place putty doughnut around fingers. Stretch loop by opening fingers.
- Pinching/poking: roll the putty into a thick snake. Place the snake on the table and pinch the edges to make a 'dinosaur/crocodile tail'. Use finger and thumb to pinch, starting with the index finger and working towards little finger.
- Making confetti: have students break apart the putty into small 'confetti' pieces by using their thumb and index finger. Once finished, roll all pieces using thumb and index finger into small balls and use tweezers to place back into container one by one.

*

BUTTONS MADE EASY

○ 132 ○

Doing some fun warm-up activities prior to handwriting practice or any activity requiring fine motor skills can help students to prepare mentally and physically. They will increase alertness levels and warm up the muscles. This routine should take no longer than five minutes.

- ◆ Start with toggles as they are good to practise with and are easier to grasp.
- ◆ Buttonholes on new shirts are often tight and may need snipping slightly to open them up or just stretching by pushing the button through and back repeatedly.
- ◆ While learning buttons, sew sleeve buttons on with elastic so the arm can be pushed straight through. Much quicker when changing for PE or dressing in the morning!
- ◆ Place a coloured sticker on the button and the same colour next to the corresponding hole to ease lining up the correct button.
- ◆ Allow students to do up those that they can see (e.g. at the bottom of a shirt). Start the task if necessary but then allow them to finish and pull the button through. Replace frequently used buttons with smaller ones (e.g. on coat or cardigan) as these will be easier to do up and are a good place to start.
- ◆ Buttons are easier to grasp if they are flat (instead of concave), large, textured or sewn slightly above the surface of the garment.

Button games

- ◆ Posting games like pennies in a piggy bank.
- ◆ Threading games with cotton reels, beads and big buttons. Work with finer and finer sizes as progress is made.
- ◆ Post pennies through a slit in a square of card or try the lid of a tub. Then use scraps of material.
- ◆ Put two big buttons on either end of a piece of elastic and thread bits of paper or material on to the elastic. Gradually make the slit smaller and smaller. Once these skills are mastered, start using garments with button holes.
- ◆ Button pieces of felt together to make a felt chain.

ZIP PRACTICE

BACKWARDS CHAINING

This means that you teach the last step first. It is a great way to encourage success. Use small steps and this will help with attention, too! As students become successful, add another step in the chain from the end of the task.

So, for zipping, start with unzipping, then you start the zipper at the bottom and the student pulls up, then hold one side of garment while the student slots in zip and then pulls up and so on.

HAND-OVER-HAND ASSISTANCE

Sometimes hand-over-hand assistance is essential. Place your hand over their hands and gently show with physical assistance how to manage the step involved.

The key is plenty of practice!

- Start to practise zips by allowing students to store items in purses, pencil cases and bags with zips where no end connection is required.
- Use zipper/ziplock wallets to store school items or small toys in.
- Add a key ring or tab to zips to help with pulling up. Lots of character zip pulls are available to buy.

*

SHOELACE TYING

○ 134 ○

Tying shoelaces is an extremely complex skill that can be very difficult to learn. There are so many different skill areas that are used when tying shoelaces. If you have difficulties in any of these areas, then tying laces will be tricky. Tying laces requires fine motor skills, good visual perception, good visual motor abilities, the ability to skilfully use two hands together, hand strength and, above all, motivation and patience!

Typical developmental milestones in this area are:

Milestone	Age (approximate)
Unties knot	2
Can pull the laces tight	3
Ties a knot	4
Ties a bow	6/6.5

Helpful tips when teaching shoelacing

◆ Practise threading laces through the holes of their shoe or through fun activities such as lacing cards. These can easily be made with some stiff card and a hole punch. Use sturdy laces and wrap tape around the end to make it easier. Shoelace tying boards can easily be made using thick card.

◆ Use sturdy laces or rope around legs to practise. Tie two different coloured ropes together to emphasise the crossover.

There are several alternatives to tying laces on the market which can be used.

STARTING KNOT

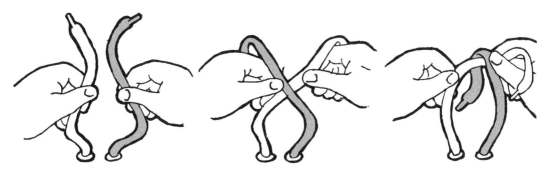

Hold one lace in each hand | Cross one over the other | Bend one lace over other, pull through the 'hole' in the middle

TIE A BOW – BUNNY EARS/TWO LOOP METHOD

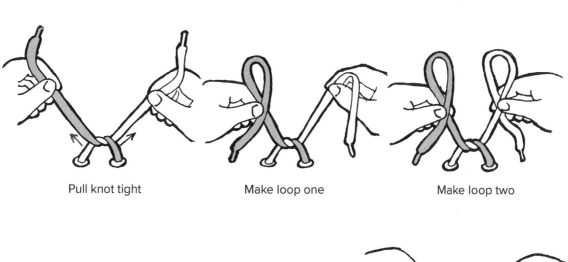

Pull knot tight | Make loop one | Make loop two

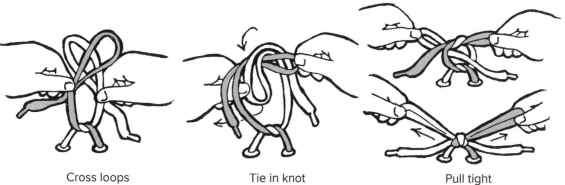

Cross loops | Tie in knot | Pull tight

WRAP AROUND METHOD

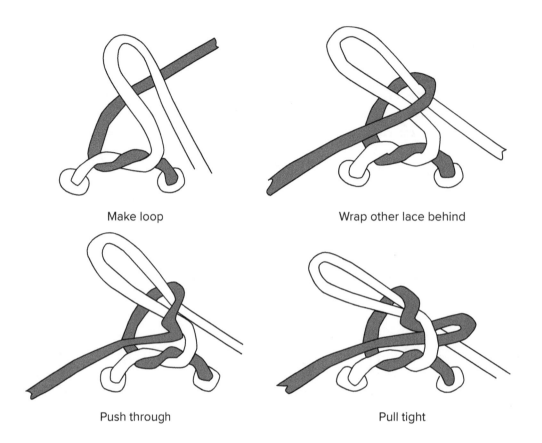

Make loop

Wrap other lace behind

Push through

Pull tight

References and further reading

Agony Autie (2018) 'Stimming | What's that?' YouTube. Accessed on 9/12/2021 at https://youtu.be/8bhT2R9HiLs.

American Psychiatric Association (2013) *Diagnostic and Statistical Manual of Mental Disorders (DSM-5)*. Arlington, VA: American Psychiatric Association.

Attwood, T. (1998) *Asperger's Syndrome: A Guide for Parents and Professionals*. London: Jessica Kingsley Publishers.

Attwood, T., Evans, C.R. and Lesko, A. (2014) *Been There. Done That. Try This! An Aspie's Guide to Life on Earth*. London: Jessica Kingsley Publishers.

Ayres, J.A. (1979) *Sensory Integration and the Child*. Torrance, CA: Western Psychological Services.

Beadle-Brown, J. and Mills, R. (2018) *Understanding and Responding to Autism: The SPELL Framework* (2nd edn). Shoreham-by-Sea: Pavilion Publishing.

Beardon, L. (2017) *Autism and Asperger Syndrome in Adults*. London: Sheldon Press.

Beale-Ellis, S. (2017) *Sensing the City: An Autistic Perspective*. London: Jessica Kingsley Publishers.

Bogdashina, O. (2003) *Sensory Perceptual Issues in Autism and Asperger Syndrome*. London: Jessica Kingsley Publishers.

Boucher, J. (2022) *Autism Spectrum Disorders: Characteristics, Causes and Practical Issues*. London: Sage.

Buron, K.D. and Curtis, M. (2012) *The Incredible 5-Point Scale: The Significantly Improved and Expanded Second Edition. Assisting Students in Understanding Social Interactions and Controlling Their Emotional Responses*. Overland Park, KS: AAPC Publishing.

DesJardins, K. (2021) *Autism: Life in the Prism*. Shawnee, KS: AAPC Publishing.

Fuentes, C.T., Mostofsky, S.H. and Bastian, A.J. (2009) 'Children with autism show specific handwriting impairments.' *Neurology 73*, 19, 1532–1537.

Gillingham, G. (1995) *Autism: Handle with Care! Understanding and Managing Behavior of Children and Adults with Autism*. Arlington, TX: Future Education Inc.

Grandin, T. (1986) *Emergence: Labelled Autistic*. New York, NY: Warner Books.

Grandin, T. (1991) 'Temple Grandin: Inside ASD.' Autism Research Institute. Accessed on 9/12/2021 at www.autism.org/temple-grandin-inside-asd.

Grandin, T. (2016) 'What we can learn about emotional regulation from Temple Grandin.' FirstPath Autism. Accessed on 9/12/2021 at https://firstpathautism.com/can-learn-emotional-regulation-temple-grandin.

Green, D., Baird, G., Barnett, A.L., Henderson, L., Huber, J. and Henderson, S.E. (2002) 'The severity and nature of motor impairment in Asperger's syndrome: A comparison with specific developmental disorder of motor function.' *Journal of Child Psychology and Psychiatry 43*, 5, 655–668.

Heller, S. (2003) *Too Loud, Too Bright, Too Fast, Too Tight: What to Do if You Are Sensory Defensive in an Over-Stimulating World*. New York, NY: HarperCollins.

Horwood, J. (2009) *Sensory Circuits: A Sensory Motor Skills Programme for Children*. Hyde: LDA.

Johnson-Ecker, C.L. and Parham, L.D. (2000) 'The evaluation of sensory processing: A validity study using contrasting groups.' *American Journal of Occupational Therapy 54*, 5, 494–503.

Koenig, K.P., Buckley-Reen, A. and Garg, S. (2012) 'Efficacy of the Get Ready to Learn yoga program among children with autism spectrum disorders: A pretest–posttest control group design.' *American Journal of Occupational Therapy 66*, 5, 538–546.

Knight, J. (n.d.) 'About us.' Accessed on 9/12/2021 at https://spacedoutandsmiling.com/about.

Krannowitz, C.S. (2005) *The Out-of-Sync Child: Recognizing and Coping with Sensory Processing Disorder* (2nd edn). New York, NY: TarcherPerigee.

Kuypers, L. (2011) *The Zones of Regulation: A Curriculum Designed to Foster Self-Regulation and Emotional Control*. Santa Clara, CA: Think Social Publishing.

Limpsfield Grange School and Martin, V. (2015) *M is for Autism*. London: Jessica Kingsley Publishers.

Mahler, K.J. (2016) *Interoception – The Eighth Sensory System: Practical Solutions for Improving Self-Regulation, Self-Awareness and Social Understanding of Individuals with Autism Spectrum and Related Disorders*. Overland Park, KS: AAPC Publishing.

Mahler, K. (2021) 'What is interoception?' Accessed on 6/12/2021 at www.kelly-mahler.com/what-is-interoception.

National Autistic Society (2020a) 'Autistic fatigue – a guide for parents and carers.' Accessed on 6/12/2021 at www.autism.org.uk/advice-and-guidance/topics/mental-health/autistic-fatigue/parents#:~:text=Changes%20in%20your%20routines%20or,to%20recover%20quickly%20from%20meltdowns.

National Autistic Society (2020b) 'Autistic fatigue – a guide for professionals.' Accessed on 6/12/2021 at www.autism.org.uk/advice-and-guidance/topics/mental-health/autistic-fatigue/professionals.

National Autistic Society (2021) 'Mental health.' Accessed on 6/12/2021 at www.autism.org.uk/about/health/mental-health.aspx.

National Eating Disorders Association (2021) 'Pica.' Accessed on 6/12/2021 at www.nationaleatingdisorders.org/learn/by-eating-disorder/other/pica.

Norwood, J. (2009) *Sensory Circuits: A Sensory Motor Skills Programme for Children*. Hyde: LDA.

O'Mahony, M. (2015) 'No two people are the same, so why should treatments for autism be? Donna Williams tells Micheál O'Mahony how she copes with autism.' Irish Examiner, 19 August. Accessed on 14/12/2021 at www.irishexaminer.com/lifestyle/arid-20348954.html.

O'Neill, J.L. (1999) *Through the Eyes of Aliens: A Book about Autistic People*. London: Jessica Kingsley Publishers.

Stehli, A. (1991) *The Sound of a Miracle: A Child's Triumph over Autism*. New York, NY: Doubleday.

Steward, R. (2013) *The Independent Woman's Handbook for Super Safe Living on the Autistic Spectrum*. London: Jessica Kingsley Publishers.

Steward, R. (2020) 'Meltdowns.' Accessed on 9/12/2021 at www.robynsteward.com/research.

Stockman, J. (2019) 'A rare view into the world of autism with Jolen Stockman.' Say Magazine, Issue 100. Accessed on 6/12/2021 at https://saymag.com/jolene-stockman.

Sunbeck, D. (2002) *The Complete Infinity Walk, Book 1: The Physical Self*. Rochester, NY: The Leonardo Foundation Press.

Williams, D. (1992) *Nobody Nowhere*. Toronto: Doubleday.

Williams, D. (1996) *Autism – An Inside-Out Approach: An Innovative Look at the Mechanisms of 'Autism' and Its Developmental 'Cousins'*. London: Jessica Kingsley Publishers.

Williams, C.M., Tinley, P. and Curtin, M. (2010) 'Idiopathic toe walking and sensory processing dysfunction.' *Journal of Foot and Ankle Research 3*, 16.

Winter, M. (2003) *Asperger Syndrome: What Teachers Need to Know*. London: Jessica Kingsley Publishers.

● USEFUL WEBSITES

Autism Education Trust – www.autismeducationtrust.org.uk

National Autistic Society – www.autism.org.uk

About the author

Corinna Laurie qualified as an occupational therapist in 1993 and has extensive experience within the areas of autism and sensory processing differences. Corinna is also skilled in a variety of paediatric evaluation tools and treatment approaches, including Sensory Integration, Therapeutic Listening® and neurodevelopmental techniques, and is certified in the use of the ADOS-2 diagnostic tool. She also has a diploma in aromatherapy and reflexology which she uses to further enhance her practice.

Corinna has worked for many years with the National Autistic Society and is the director of Evolve-Children's Therapy Services Ltd, which specialises in treatment and assessment for children with sensory processing differences and physical disabilities. In addition, Corinna provides clinical training to a variety of settings and presents nationally to a wide variety of audiences.